HOME DISTILLING FOR BEGINNERS

A step by step guide to making your own fine spirits at home with easy to follow process, essential tips and mouthwatering recipes

© MATTEO CONTI

TABLE OF CONTENTS

INTRODUCTION 4

A brief history of distilling................................4

The resurgence of home distilling..........................7

Overview of the book content...............................10

CHAPTER ONE - THE FUNDAMENTALS OF HOME DISTILLATION
....12

The science behind distillation 12

Vaporization and Condensation: The Driving Forces of
Distillation..15

The Role of Fractional Distillation in Purification.........16

Safety Considerations in Distillation 18

Equipment and tools required for home distilling............19

CHAPTER 2. BASIC TECHNIQUES AND PROCESSES..................28

A step-by-step guide to the distillation process 28

Mashing and Fermentation 32

Yeast Selection and Fermentation Methods 33

CHAPTER 3. VODKA: FROM GRAIN TO BOTTLE....................37

Understanding vodka production 37

Recipes and Techniques for Grain-based Vodka..............40

Infusing Vodka with Flavors..............................41

Filtering and Bottling Vodka 43

CHAPTER FOUR - WHISKEY: THE ART OF AGING AND FLAVOR..46

Different Types of Whiskey...............................46

Mash Preparation 49

Aging and Maturation..55

Quality Assessment..59

CHAPTER 5-DISTILLING FRUITS INTO ELEGANCE 66

Distillation and how they are applied in brandy production. 67

Fruit Selection and Fermentation 69

Blending and Artistry 75

Tasting and Appreciation 82

CHAPTER 6-TROUBLESHOOTING AND COMMON MISTAKES.....85

Troubleshooting Distillation Problems 88

Tasting and Sampling..90

CHAPTER 7- SAFETY, LEGALITIES, AND RESPONSIBLE DISTILLING 92

Ensuring Safety during the Distillation Process 92

Legal regulations and permits for home distilling 97

Responsible Consumption and Sharing of Homemade Spirits 102

Ethical Considerations in distillation....................................105

Guidelines for Responsible Drinking....................................110

CONCLUSION 128

INTRODUCTION

A brief history of distilling

In the realms of human civilization, few pursuits have captivated our senses and stimulated our imagination as profoundly as the art of distilling. From the ancient alchemists seeking the elixir of life to the modern-day connoisseurs perfecting their craft, distillation has woven its way into the fabric of our history. In this chapter, we embark on a journey through time, unraveling the captivating tapestry of distilling's remarkable evolution. In order to truly understand the roots of distilling, we must venture back to the dawn of human ingenuity. The origins of distillation are veiled in the mists of time, with evidence suggesting its existence as early as 2,000 BCE in Mesopotamia and ancient Egypt. However, it was in the cradle of civilization, the Fertile Crescent, where the art of distillation began to take shape.

Distilling emerged from the alchemists' insatiable quest to transmute base metals into precious gold and discover the mythical elixir of life. While their ambitions remained unfulfilled, their tireless experiments with potions, tinctures, and distillates laid the foundation for the art of distillation. The alchemists' unwavering pursuit of knowledge and their dedication to uncovering the secrets of the universe set the stage for future generations of distillers. In the 8th century, the Islamic Golden Age ushered in an era of great progress and innovation in various fields, including distillation. The Arab scholars, building upon the knowledge inherited from the alchemists, made significant advancements in the art. They introduced the alembic, an ingenious distillation apparatus consisting of a pot, a condenser, and a collection vessel. With this device, they refined the process, allowing for a more precise separation of spirits and the creation of concentrated aromatic essences.

As the medieval era descended upon Europe, distillation became intertwined with the everyday lives of its inhabitants. Monastic orders, particularly those within the Christian tradition, played a pivotal role in nurturing the distillation arts during this time. In the hallowed halls of monastic distilleries, the knowledge of distillation was preserved and further developed. Monks distilled medicinal herbal remedies, elixirs, and spirits for both therapeutic and sacramental purposes. Their meticulous record-keeping and experimentation paved the way for the refinement of distilling techniques and the gradual expansion of spirit production beyond the monastery walls. By the 13th century, the distilled spirit known as "aqua vitae" (water of life) gained popularity across Europe. This potent elixir was believed to possess curative properties, ward off disease, and invigorate the spirit. Aqua vitae became an integral part of medieval society, shaping social customs and establishing a foundation for the vibrant spirit culture that would follow in the centuries to come.

The advent of the Industrial Revolution in the 18th century brought about profound changes in the world of distilling. Innovations in technology, such as the invention of column stills and continuous distillation methods, revolutionized the production process and paved the way for the mass production of spirits.Scotland, with its bountiful fields of barley and pristine water sources, emerged as the epicenter of whiskey production. The introduction of continuous still and aging techniques allowed Scottish distillers to produce whiskey on a larger scale while maintaining quality and consistency. The reputation of Scottish whiskey quickly spread across borders, captivating the palates of connoisseurs worldwide. The early 20th century brought with it a tumultuous period known as Prohibition, during which the production, sale, and distribution of alcoholic beverages were prohibited in the United States. However, this era of restriction and illicit activities also fueled the ingenuity of home-distillers. Under the veil of darkness, hidden stills produced moonshine and bootlegged spirits, defying the law and satisfying the thirst of those seeking a forbidden indulgence. Although Prohibition eventually came to an end, its impact on the clandestine art of distilling would forever be etched in history.

In recent years, there has been a resurgence of interest in home distilling. As laws and regulations have evolved in various countries, enthusiasts now have the opportunity to explore the craft of distilling within the comfort of their own homes. This resurgence can be attributed to a desire for experimentation, the quest for unique flavors, and the satisfaction of creating spirits with a personal touch. The history of distilling is an extraordinary tale woven with threads of human curiosity, scientific discovery, and cultural heritage. From the alchemists' pursuit of transmutation to the monastic distilleries and the modern craft distillers, each chapter in the story of distilling has contributed to the rich tapestry of spirits that we enjoy today. As we embark on this journey through the art of home distilling, we honor the legacy of those who came before us and embrace the opportunity to craft our own spirits, steeped in tradition yet infused with our own creative flair. In this book, we will delve deeper into the techniques, ingredients, and nuances of distilling as we explore the world of vodka, whiskey, and brandy. So, grab a glass, raise it in a toast to the past, and let us embark on this captivating voyage through the realms of homemade spirits.

The resurgence of home distilling

In recent years, an enchanting revival has taken place in the realm of distilling, as enthusiasts around the world have rekindled the age-old tradition of crafting spirits within the comfort of their own homes. The resurgence of home distilling has captivated the imaginations of individuals seeking to explore their creativity, embrace the art of flavor experimentation, and savor the unique satisfaction of producing spirits that are a true reflection of their personal tastes. In this chapter, we embark on a journey to uncover the reasons behind this remarkable resurgence and delve into the captivating world of home distilling. One of the key factors contributing to the resurgence of home distilling is the gradual easing of legal restrictions in many countries. While laws and regulations regarding the production of spirits vary widely across jurisdictions, an increasing number of regions have recognized the desire of enthusiasts to explore the craft within their own homes. As a result, home distillers now have access to a wider range of equipment, ingredients, and resources, fostering an environment conducive to their creative endeavors.

The rise of the craft distilling movement has played a significant role in reshaping the perception of homemade spirits. Craft distillers, with their emphasis on quality, craftsmanship, and attention to detail, have inspired home enthusiasts to embrace their own distilling journeys. By showcasing the potential for unique flavor profiles and the artistry involved in spirit production, craft distillers have not only elevated the standards of the industry but also motivated individuals to embark on their own creative distilling ventures. Home distilling provides a platform for individuals to explore their creativity and experiment with flavors in ways that commercial spirits may not offer. By crafting their own spirits, home distillers can tailor taste experiences to their personal preferences, creating products that are truly unique and reflective of their individual palates. This freedom to experiment with different grains, fruits, herbs, and spices allows for an infinite variety of flavor possibilities, making the journey of home distilling an exciting and deeply personal one. For many, home distilling represents an opportunity to engage in an artisanal craft, combining science, tradition, and personal skill. From selecting the finest ingredients to carefully monitoring the distillation process, home distillers embrace the role of master craftsmen, ensuring every step is executed with precision and care. This hands-on approach fosters a deep sense of pride and satisfaction as they witness the transformation of raw materials into refined spirits, making the entire process a truly rewarding endeavor.

The digital age has brought together a vibrant community of home distillers, providing platforms for knowledge sharing, recipe exchange, and the celebration of successes. Online forums, social media groups, and dedicated websites offer a wealth of information, tips, and tricks, creating a virtual space where enthusiasts can connect, learn from one another, and inspire new creations. This sense of community fosters a supportive environment, encouraging novices to embark on their own distilling journeys while providing a valuable resource for experienced distillers to expand their repertoire. The growing interest in home distilling has led to an increase in educational opportunities and workshops where enthusiasts can further hone their skills and deepen their understanding of the craft. Experienced distillers, industry professionals, and experts in the field offer insights into the science behind distillation, the nuances of flavor development, and the legal aspects of home distilling. These educational initiatives not only empower individuals to embark on their own distilling ventures with confidence but also promote responsible and informed practices within the home distilling community.

The resurgence of home distilling is intertwined with a broader cultural movement toward appreciating handcrafted, artisanal products. In a world saturated with mass-produced goods, there is a growing desire for products that reflect a sense of authenticity, craftsmanship, and attention to detail. Home distilling allows individuals to reclaim a connection with the art of spirit production, emphasizing quality over quantity and embracing the satisfaction that comes from creating something truly exceptional with their own hands. Home distilling provides an avenue for individuals to embrace sustainability and support local producers. Many home distillers opt to source their ingredients from nearby farms, orchards, or gardens, reducing their carbon footprint and fostering a sense of community engagement. By utilizing fresh, seasonal produce and supporting local suppliers, home distillers contribute to the preservation of traditional farming practices and promote a more sustainable approach to spirit production.

The resurgence of home distilling has breathed new life into the art and craft of spirit production. Driven by a changing legal landscape, a desire for creativity and personal expression, a sense of community, and a return to craftsmanship and quality, enthusiasts around the world have embraced the joys and challenges of producing their own spirits at home. As we venture further into this book, we will explore the techniques, recipes, and intricacies of crafting vodka, whiskey, and brandy, empowering readers to embark on their own distilling journeys. So raise your glass and join us as we celebrate the resurgence of home distilling, where creativity, flavor, and passion intertwine to create spirits that are truly one of a kind.

Overview of the book content
Welcome to the captivating world of home distilling, where creativity, flavor exploration, and the pursuit of craftsmanship converge. In this comprehensive guide, we invite you to embark on a journey that will unlock the secrets and techniques behind the art of

distillation. Whether you're a novice enthusiast or an experienced home distiller, this book is designed to inspire, educate, and empower you to create your own exceptional spirits. Get ready to delve into the intriguing history of distilling, from its ancient origins to the modern resurgence of the craft. Discover how alchemists, monks, and innovators have shaped the art of distillation throughout the ages, setting the stage for the home-distilling revolution that we are witnessing today.

As you embark on this exciting voyage through the world of home distilling, be prepared to unleash your creativity, engage your senses, and embark on a path of mastery. From the rich history of distillation to the technical intricacies of crafting vodka, whiskey, and brandy, this book serves as your trusted companion, guiding you through the art and science of creating exceptional spirits. Whether you're seeking to impress friends with unique cocktails or simply savor the satisfaction of crafting your own spirits, let the adventure begin. Cheers to the joy of home distilling!

CHAPTER ONE - THE FUNDAMENTALS OF HOME DISTILLATION

The science behind distillation

Distillation is a fascinating process that allows us to separate different components of a liquid mixture based on their boiling points. At its core, distillation capitalizes on the fact that different substances have varying boiling points, and by manipulating temperature and pressure, we can selectively vaporize and condense these substances to obtain a purified product. The fundamental principle behind distillation is simple: when a mixture is heated, the component with the lowest boiling point vaporizes first. The vapor is then collected and condensed back into a liquid, resulting in a separation of the desired substance from the impurities or other unwanted components.

Temperature plays a crucial role in distillation. By carefully controlling the temperature, we can control which substances vaporize and which remain in the liquid phase. In a typical distillation setup, a heat source is applied to the mixture, raising its temperature. As the temperature increases, the substance with the lowest boiling point will start to vaporize. This vapor contains molecules of the desired substance, along with other volatile components present in the mixture. The vapor then rises through the distillation apparatus, leaving behind the nonvolatile or less volatile substances. Vaporization occurs when the heat energy provided to the liquid overcomes the intermolecular forces holding the molecules together. As the molecules gain enough energy, they break free from the liquid phase and enter the gaseous phase, forming the vapor. The vapor is then led into a condensation apparatus, where it is cooled down. Cooling the vapor causes a decrease in temperature, allowing the molecules to lose their thermal energy and return to the liquid phase. This process is known as condensation.

During condensation, the vapor undergoes a phase change and transforms back into a liquid. The liquid that is collected after condensation is referred to as the distillate, which ideally contains a higher concentration of the desired substance compared to the original mixture. The role of temperature, vaporization, and condensation in distillation is intertwined. By carefully controlling the temperature at various stages of the distillation process, we can selectively vaporize the desired substance and then condense it to obtain a purified product.

Moreover, the design of the distillation apparatus, such as the type still used, can influence the efficiency and effectiveness of the separation process. Different stills, such as pot stills or reflux stills, offer varying degrees of control over temperature and condensation, allowing for tailored distillation processes to produce specific types of spirits. Understanding the science behind distillation empowers home distillers to refine their techniques and create high-quality vodka, whiskey, brandy, and other spirits with exceptional flavor profiles. By mastering the principles of distillation and manipulating temperature, vaporization, and condensation, you can embark on a journey of crafting your own unique and artisanal beverages at home. Remember, however, that distillation of alcohol at home may be subject to legal regulations in your jurisdiction. It is essential to familiarize yourself with local laws and obtain any necessary permits or licenses before engaging in home distillation activities.

Temperature control is vital in distillation because it directly influences the separation and purity of the distilled product. The temperature at which a substance boils is unique to each compound, known as its boiling point. By carefully adjusting the temperature during distillation, we can selectively vaporize and separate the desired substance while leaving behind impurities. To achieve precise temperature control, distillation setups often incorporate a heat source, such as a burner or electric heating element, along with a temperature monitoring device, such as a thermometer or temperature sensor. This allows the distiller to regulate the heat input and maintain the desired temperature range.

During distillation, it is crucial to operate within a specific temperature range, known as the boiling point range of the desired substance. The boiling point range indicates the temperature at which the substance starts to vaporize and the temperature at which it fully condenses. By maintaining the temperature within this range, we can optimize the separation process and obtain a purer distillate. The boiling point range is influenced by factors such as the atmospheric pressure and the composition of the mixture being distilled. Lowering the atmospheric pressure, for example, can lower the boiling points of substances, making it easier to separate them. This principle is utilized in vacuum distillation, where reduced pressure allows for distillation at lower temperatures, minimizing the chances of heat-induced degradation. In addition to the boiling point range, it is essential to consider the impact of temperature gradients within the distillation apparatus. Variations in temperature throughout the setup can lead to uneven vaporization and condensation, affecting the overall quality of the distillate. Proper insulation and heat distribution techniques can help minimize temperature gradients and ensure a more consistent distillation process.

Vaporization and Condensation: The Driving Forces of Distillation

Vaporization and condensation are the two fundamental processes that facilitate the separation of substances in distillation. Understanding these processes is key to mastering the art of home distillation. Vaporization, as mentioned earlier, occurs when the molecules of a substance gain sufficient energy to overcome intermolecular forces and transition from the liquid to the gaseous phase. This process primarily depends on the boiling point of the compound. Substances with lower boiling points will vaporize more readily than those with higher boiling points. To enhance vaporization, it is essential to maximize the surface area exposed to the heat source. This can be achieved through techniques such as using a reflux column or packing the distillation column with materials that increase the surface area, such as copper mesh or ceramic raschig rings. By increasing the surface area, more molecules come into contact with the heat source, promoting efficient vaporization.

Condensation, on the other hand, involves the conversion of vapor back into liquid as it cools down. This process occurs when the temperature of the vapor is reduced to a point where the molecular energy decreases and intermolecular forces become dominant, causing the molecules to reassemble into a liquid state. Efficient condensation is crucial to collect a purified distillate. Cooling methods like water condensers or air-cooled condensers are used to bring down the temperature of the vapor, facilitating its transition back to a liquid. The design and efficiency of the condensation apparatus play a significant role in the overall distillation process.

By harnessing the principles of vaporization and condensation, home distillers can separate and concentrate the desired components, such as ethanol in the case of alcoholic beverages, while leaving behind impurities. This enables the production of spirits with enhanced flavors, aromas, and overall quality. Understanding the science behind distillation, including temperature control, vaporization, and condensation, empowers aspiring home distillers to create exceptional spirits. By mastering these principles, they can refine their distillation techniques and achieve consistent results with each batch of vodka, whiskey, brandy, or other spirits they produce.

The Role of Fractional Distillation in Purification

Fractional distillation is an advanced distillation technique commonly used to achieve higher purity levels in the distillate. It involves multiple vaporization and condensation steps within a fractionating column, which contains plates or packing material to facilitate the separation of different components based on their boiling points. In fractional distillation, the column is designed to create a temperature gradient, with lower temperatures at the top and higher temperatures at the bottom. As the vapor rises through the column, it encounters surfaces or packing material that provide additional opportunities for vaporization and condensation.

The surfaces or packing material in the fractionating column serve two purposes. Firstly, they increase the contact area between the vapor and the liquid, enhancing the separation of volatile compounds. Secondly, they create a series of vapor and liquid phases, allowing for repeated cycles of vaporization and condensation. This enables the separation of substances with boiling points that are closer together. As the vapor rises through the column, substances with lower boiling points will vaporize more readily and ascend higher before condensing. On the other hand, substances with higher boiling points will condense and trickle down the column to be collected separately. This continuous cycling of vaporization and condensation enriches the distillate with the desired components and helps remove impurities or unwanted compounds.

Fractional distillation is particularly effective when dealing with complex mixtures or when a higher level of purification is desired. It allows for the separation of azeotropic mixtures, which are mixtures that boil at a constant temperature, making them difficult to separate by simple distillation. By employing a fractionating column, home distillers can achieve greater control over the distillation process and produce spirits with exceptional purity.

Safety Considerations in Distillation

While the science behind distillation is fascinating, it is essential to emphasize safety precautions when engaging in home distillation. Distillation involves heating flammable substances and working with potentially hazardous equipment, so it is crucial to prioritize safety to prevent accidents or injuries.

Here are some key safety considerations for home distillation:

- Ensure proper ventilation in your distillation area to prevent the buildup of flammable vapors. Distillation should be conducted in well-ventilated spaces or with the use of fume hoods.
- Use suitable heat sources and equipment designed for distillation. Avoid open flames and opt for electric heating elements or specialized distillation equipment.
- Familiarize yourself with the properties of the substances you are distilling, including their flammability and toxicity. Follow all safety

guidelines and handling procedures for these substances.

- Always monitor and control the temperature during distillation to prevent overheating or excessive pressure buildup.
- Regularly inspect and maintain your distillation apparatus to ensure its integrity and functionality. Replace any damaged or worn-out components.
- Educate yourself on the legal regulations regarding home distillation in your jurisdiction. Adhere to any licensing requirements or restrictions to ensure compliance with the law.

By prioritizing safety and taking necessary precautions, home distillers can enjoy the process of distillation while minimizing risks and creating a safe environment for themselves and others.

Understanding the science behind distillation, including temperature control, vaporization, condensation, fractional distillation, and safety considerations, lays a solid foundation for aspiring home-distillers. Armed with this knowledge, you can embark on your journey of crafting high-quality spirits, experimenting with different ingredients, and honing your distillation skills to create unique and delightful beverages at home.

Equipment and tools required for home distilling

When it comes to home distilling, having the right equipment and tools is crucial for achieving successful and safe distillation results. Each component plays a significant role in the distillation process, from heating the mixture to collecting the distillate. Let's explore the essential equipment and tools necessary for home distillation and understand their importance in producing high-quality spirits.

Distillation Apparatus

The distillation apparatus is the core component of any home distillation setup. It typically consists of the following key elements:

I.   Still

The still is the central vessel where the distillation process takes place. There are different types of stills available, each with its own advantages and purposes. The two most commonly used stills for home distillation are pot stills and reflux stills.

Choosing the right type of still depends on the desired outcome and the specific spirits you intend to produce. Consider factors such as flavor profiles, purity requirements, and personal preferences when selecting a still for your home distillation endeavors.

II.   Condenser

The condenser is an essential component of the distillation apparatus that cools down the vapor, causing it to condense back into a liquid. It consists of a pipe or coil through which cold water or air is circulated, reducing the temperature of the vapor. There are different types of condensers, such as water condensers and air-cooled condensers. Water condensers use a flow of cold water to cool the vapor, while air-cooled condensers utilize ambient air for cooling. Choosing the appropriate condenser depends on factors like available resources, personal preferences, and the specific requirements of your distillation setup.

III.   Heating Source

A reliable and controllable heat source is crucial for initiating the vaporization process during distillation. There are several options available for home distillers:

IV.   Electric Heating Element

Electric heating elements, such as hotplates or electric coils, are commonly used for home distillation setups. They provide consistent heat and temperature control, ensuring precision during the distillation process. Electric heating elements are safer and more convenient to use compared to open flames, making them a popular choice among home-distillers.

V.   Gas Burner

Gas burners, such as propane or natural gas burners, are another option for heating the distillation apparatus. They offer higher heat output, allowing for faster heating of the mixture. However, it is important to exercise caution when using gas burners due to the open flame and the potential risks associated with them. Always follow safety guidelines and operate gas burners in a well-ventilated area.

VI.   Thermometer or Temperature Sensor

Accurate temperature measurement is crucial in controlling the distillation process. A thermometer or temperature sensor is an indispensable tool for monitoring and maintaining the temperature within the desired range. It allows the distiller to make necessary adjustments to the heat source and ensure optimal conditions for vaporization and condensation. There are various types of thermometers and temperature sensors available, including analog thermometers, digital thermometers, and infrared temperature guns. Choose a thermometer or temperature sensor that is suitable for the specific requirements of your distillation setup and provides accurate readings within the desired temperature range.

VII.   Collection Vessels

Collection vessels are used to collect the distilled product, also known as the distillate, during the distillation process. These vessels can vary in size and material, depending on the volume of distillate produced and personal preferences. Common options for collection vessels include glass containers, stainless steel containers, or food-grade plastic containers. It is important to choose collection vessels that are resistant to chemical reactions and can withstand the temperatures involved in distillation. Ensure that the vessels are clean, sterile, and properly sealed to maintain the integrity and quality of the distilled product.

Importance of Choosing the Right Equipment and Ingredients for Successful Distillation

Selecting the appropriate equipment and ingredients is crucial for achieving successful distillation and producing high-quality spirits. Here's why it matters:

Equipment Quality and Efficiency

Using high-quality distillation equipment ensures better control over the distillation process, resulting in improved efficiency and consistent results. Well-designed stills and condensers, along with reliable heating sources and temperature measurement tools, contribute to a more precise and controlled distillation environment.

Investing in good-quality equipment also enhances safety during distillation. It reduces the risks associated with equipment failures, such as leaks or overheating, which can lead to accidents or compromised results.

The choice of ingredients, especially the base material or "wash," significantly impacts the flavor, aroma, and overall character of the distilled spirits. For example, the selection of grains for whiskey or fruits for brandy can greatly influence the final product's taste and quality. Opting for high-quality ingredients is essential to ensure that the flavors and characteristics of the spirits are not compromised. Use fresh, ripe fruits or premium-grade grains to achieve the desired flavor profiles in your spirits.

Moreover, it is important to source ingredients that are free from any contaminants or impurities that could negatively affect the distillation process or the quality of the final product. This includes ensuring the absence of pesticides, chemicals, or any other substances that may be harmful or alter the intended flavors of the spirits.

By choosing the right equipment and ingredients, home distillers can elevate their distillation process and create spirits of exceptional quality. Careful consideration of equipment quality, functionality, and safety features, combined with the use of high-quality ingredients, paves the way for successful and rewarding home distilling experiences. Remember, it is essential to comply with legal regulations and obtain any necessary permits or licenses related to home distillation in your jurisdiction. Always prioritize safety, follow best practices, and enjoy the art and science of distillation responsibly.

Understanding the Different Types of Stills

Stills are the heart of the distillation process, providing the environment where the transformation of a liquid mixture into vapor and subsequent condensation occur. Different types of stills are available, each offering unique advantages and characteristics that influence the final outcome of the distillation process. Let's explore the most common types of stills used in home distillation and understand their distinct features. So, in simple terms, a still is a special machine that heats up a mixture, turns it into vapor, cools down the vapor, and collects the liquid that forms. It helps separate different components based on their boiling points, allowing you to extract specific liquids, like alcohol, from a mixture.

- **Pot Still**

The pot still is a classic and versatile type of still that has been used for centuries to produce a wide range of spirits. It consists of a large pot or boiler, a swan neck or lyne arm, and a condenser. The pot still is known for its simplicity and its ability to retain and impart flavors from the ingredients used.

When the mixture is heated in the pot, vapor rises through the swan neck and enters the condenser, where it is cooled and collected as distillate. The pot still allows for a more direct and straightforward distillation process, preserving the flavors and aromas of the base material. Pot stills are particularly well-suited for the production of spirits like whiskey, brandy, and rum, where the emphasis is on capturing the character of the raw ingredients. The shape and size of the pot still can also influence the final product, with different designs producing variations in flavor and quality.

- **Reflux Still**

Reflux still, also known as a fractionating still, is designed for achieving higher purity and separating components with closer boiling points. It incorporates a fractionating column, which can be either packed with material or contain plates. The column facilitates multiple vaporization and condensation cycles, allowing for more efficient separation of substances.

In a reflux still, vapor rises through the fractionating column, and as it ascends, it encounters surfaces or packing material that promote condensation. The condensed liquid then falls back down, creating a reflux action where vapor and liquid continuously interact. This reflux action improves the separation of volatile compounds and results in a higher-purity distillate. Reflux stills are commonly used for producing neutral spirits like vodka, where the focus is on achieving a clean and pure base alcohol that can be further flavored or used as a base for other spirits. They are known for their ability to remove impurities and produce a high-quality, smooth distillate.

- **Hybrid Still**

As the name suggests, a hybrid still combines elements of both pot stills and reflux stills. It offers the versatility of producing a wide range of spirits while providing the opportunity for better control over the distillation process. A hybrid still typically includes a pot still component, allowing for the retention of flavors and aromas, as well as a fractionating column for additional purification. The design may vary, with some hybrid stills incorporating removable or adjustable column sections, providing flexibility to the distiller. With a hybrid still, home distillers have the freedom to experiment and create spirits with varying levels of purity and flavor complexity. This versatility makes hybrid stills a popular choice for those who enjoy the art of distillation and want the ability to produce a diverse range of spirits.

Choosing the Right Still for Your Needs

When selecting a still for home distillation, several factors should be considered. These include:

- **Intended spirits**: Determine the type of spirits you wish to produce. If you prefer spirits with distinct flavors and aromas, a pot still may be the best choice. If you aim for high-purity spirits or plan to experiment with flavorings later in the process, a reflux or hybrid might still be more suitable.
- **Personal preferences:** Consider your distillation goals, the level of control you desire, and your experience level. Different still types offer varying levels of control and require different skill sets. Choose a skill that aligns with your preferences and expertise.
- **Space and budget**: Consider the available space in your distillation area and your budget constraints. Pot stills tend to be simpler in design and generally more affordable, while reflux stills can be more complex and may require additional equipment or materials.
- **Legal regulations**: Familiarize yourself with the legal regulations surrounding home distillation in your jurisdiction. Some regions may have restrictions on the types of stills that can be used or require permits for certain still designs. Ensure that your chosen still complies with all relevant laws and regulations.

Regardless of the type of still you choose, it is important to invest in a high-quality, well-built apparatus. Look for stills made from food-grade materials that are resistant to corrosion and can withstand the rigors of the distillation process. Proper maintenance and regular cleaning are essential to ensure the longevity and performance of your still.

Understanding the different types of stills empowers home distillers to make informed decisions when it comes to selecting the most suitable equipment for their distillation endeavors. Whether you opt for a pot still, reflux still, or hybrid still, each type offers unique advantages and opportunities for crafting exceptional spirits. So, explore the options, embrace the art and science of distillation, and embark on your journey to create your own signature libations.

CHAPTER 2. BASIC TECHNIQUES AND PROCESSES

A step-by-step guide to the distillation process
Distillation is a fascinating and essential process in the art of home distilling. It allows you to separate alcohol from a fermented mixture and create your own spirits with distinct flavors and characteristics. In this step-by-step guide, we will walk you through the distillation process, from setup to collecting your final product.

- **Step 1: Setup and Preparation**

Before you begin the distillation process, ensure that you have a well-maintained still and all the necessary equipment. The still typically consists of a boiling vessel, a condenser, and a collection vessel. Additionally, make sure you have a reliable heat source, such as a stove or an electric hot plate.

- **Step 2: Charge the Still**

The first step is to charge the still with your fermented mixture, also known as the wash. This can be a mash of grains, fruits, or other sources that have undergone the fermentation process. Carefully pour the wash into the boiling vessel of the still, ensuring not to spill or waste any of the valuable liquid.

- **Step 3: Heat Wash**

Once the wash is in the boiling vessel, apply gentle heat to initiate the distillation process. It is crucial to heat the wash slowly and steadily, as rapid heating can lead to a poor-quality distillate. Use a thermometer to monitor the temperature and aim to raise it gradually to around 173°F (78°C).

- **Step 4: Vaporization and Condensation**

As the wash heats up, the alcohol and other volatile compounds will vaporize and rise through the still. This vapor then enters the condenser, a coiled tube or column that is kept cool. The condenser can be cooled with water or by using a fan-assisted air cooling system. As the vapor passes through the condenser, it begins to condense back into a liquid.

- **Step 5: Collecting the Distillate**

The condensed liquid, also known as the distillate, will flow out of the condenser into the collection vessel. It is important to collect the distillate in separate fractions: the heads, hearts, and tails.

- **Step 6: Separating the Heads, Hearts, and Tails**

The heads are the initial portion of the distillate and contain volatile compounds that are undesirable for consumption. These compounds, such as methanol, have lower boiling points than ethanol and can be harmful if consumed in high concentrations. Collect the heads separately and discard them. The hearts, which come after the heads, contain the desirable ethanol and flavorful compounds that give your spirit its distinct character. Collect the hearts in a separate container, as this is the portion you will use for your final product.

The tails follow the hearts and consist of heavier compounds and fusel oils. While they may add some flavor to your spirit, they can also introduce off-notes and harshness. Collect the tails separately, as you may choose to re-distill them in future batches or use them for other purposes.

- **Step 7: Repeat and Refine**

Once you have collected the desired hearts, you can choose to repeat the distillation process to further refine your spirit. This process, known as double distillation, can enhance the purity and smoothness of your final product. It involves taking the hearts and distilling them again to separate any remaining impurities.

Cleaning and Maintenance of the Still

After completing the distillation process, it is crucial to clean and maintain your still properly. Regular cleaning helps prevent contamination and ensures the longevity of your equipment. Use a non-abrasive cleaner and warm water to clean the still thoroughly, paying attention to all the components.

Remember to always follow safety precautions during the distillation process to ensure a smooth and enjoyable home distilling experience. Here are a few essential tips for cleaning and maintaining your still:

- **Disassemble the Still**: Carefully disassemble the still, taking note of the different components, such as the boiling vessel, condenser, and collection vessel. This will allow for a thorough cleaning of each part.

- **Rinse with Warm Water**: Start by rinsing all the components with warm water to remove any residue or leftover distillate. Use a gentle stream of water to ensure thorough cleaning.
- **Use a Non-Abrasive Cleaner**: Choose a non-abrasive cleaner specifically designed for use with distilling equipment. Avoid harsh chemicals or abrasive materials that can damage the surfaces of your still. Follow the manufacturer's instructions for the cleaner and apply it to the components as recommended.
- **Scrub and Rinse:** Gently scrub the surfaces of the components with a soft sponge or cloth to remove any stubborn residue. Pay close attention to areas where buildup might occur, such as inside the condenser or around seals. Rinse each part thoroughly to remove any traces of the cleaner.
- **Check for Damage or Wear:** While cleaning, inspect the still for any signs of damage or wear. Look for cracks, leaks, or loose fittings. Replace any damaged parts to ensure the proper functioning of your still.
- **Dry Thoroughly:** After cleaning, allow each component to air dry completely before reassembling the still. Make sure there is no moisture left, as it can lead to mold or bacterial growth.
- **Store in a Clean and Dry Place:** Once dry, store your still in a clean and dry place, protected from dust and contaminants.

Consider covering the still with a cloth or a protective bag to prevent any potential debris from entering.

- **Regular Maintenance:** In addition to proper cleaning, perform regular maintenance on your still. This includes checking and replacing any worn-out gaskets or seals, ensuring the heating element is functioning correctly, and inspecting all connections and fittings for tightness.

By following these cleaning and maintenance practices, you can maintain the quality and efficiency of your still, allowing you to produce exceptional spirits consistently.

Remember, safety should always be a top priority when engaging in home distilling. Familiarize yourself with local regulations and laws regarding distillation, and ensure proper ventilation and fire safety measures are in place. Always distill in a well-ventilated area and avoid open flames or sparks that can ignite flammable vapors.

With a well-maintained still and a thorough understanding of the distillation process, you are ready to embark on the exciting journey of creating your own vodka, whiskey, brandy, and other spirits right in the comfort of your home.

Mashing and Fermentation

Mashing and fermentation are integral steps in the art of home distilling. This is where the magic begins, as you transform your chosen grains, fruits, or other sources into a flavorful liquid that will eventually become your homemade vodka, whiskey, brandy, or other spirits. In this section, we will delve into the process of mashing and fermentation, exploring the steps involved and offering insights on grain selection, yeast selection, fermentation methods, as well as monitoring and controlling the fermentation process.

Choosing Grains, Fruits, or Other Sources

The choice of ingredients for your mash greatly influences the flavor profile and character of your final spirit. When it comes to grains, popular options include barley, corn, rye, and wheat. Each grain imparts its unique characteristics, so consider experimenting with different combinations to achieve the desired flavor.

For those interested in fruit-based spirits, fruits such as apples, grapes, peaches, or even berries can be used. The choice of fruit will significantly impact the aroma and taste of the final product. Additionally, alternative sources like potatoes or sugar can be used to create different types of spirits. Be adventurous and open to exploring a wide range of possibilities.

Yeast Selection and Fermentation Methods

Yeast is a key player in the fermentation process, as it converts the sugars present in the mash into alcohol. Different yeast strains can contribute distinct flavors and aromas to the final product. It is essential to choose a yeast that complements the desired characteristics of your spirit. There are various types of yeast available, including specialized strains specifically designed for distilling. These strains can withstand higher alcohol concentrations and produce flavors suitable for spirits. Research different yeast options, and consider experimenting with different strains to discover your preferred flavor profile.

Fermentation methods can vary depending on the ingredients and equipment available. The two main approaches are traditional fermentation and controlled fermentation.

Traditional fermentation involves allowing the mash to naturally ferment with the ambient yeasts and bacteria present in the environment. This method can result in unique flavors and complexities, but it also carries the risk of inconsistent or unpredictable outcomes.

Controlled fermentation, on the other hand, involves using a specific yeast strain and maintaining optimal fermentation conditions. This method provides more control over the fermentation process, resulting in a more consistent and predictable outcome. It is achieved by closely monitoring and adjusting factors such as temperature, pH levels, and nutrient additions throughout the fermentation process.

Monitoring and Controlling the Fermentation Process

Monitoring and controlling the fermentation process is crucial to achieving a successful outcome. Here are some key factors to consider:

a) Temperature: Yeast is sensitive to temperature, so maintaining a consistent and appropriate fermentation temperature is essential. The ideal range will vary depending on the yeast strain used. Generally, temperatures between 68°F and 86°F (20°C and 30°C) are suitable for most distilling yeasts. Use a thermometer to monitor and adjust the temperature as needed.

b) pH Levels: The pH level of the mash can affe
yeast activity and fermentation. Aim for a pH
range of 4.5 to 5.5, as this provides an optimal
environment for yeast growth and sugar
conversion. Use pH test strips or a pH meter to
monitor and adjust the pH levels if necessary.

c) Nutrient Additions: Yeast requires nutrients to
thrive and carry out fermentation efficiently.
Certain nutrients, such as yeast energizers or
yeast nutrients, can be added to the mash to
ensure a healthy fermentation. Follow the
manufacturer's instructions for the proper
dosage and timing of nutrient additions.

d) Airlock and Fermentation Vessel: During
fermentation, carbon dioxide is released. To
prevent contamination and allow gas to escape,
fit your fermentation vessel with an airlock. An
airlock is a device that allows carbon dioxide to
exit the vessel while preventing air or
contaminants from entering. It helps maintain
a controlled and sanitary environment for
fermentation.

e) Fermentation Duration: The duration of
fermentation can vary depending on factors
such as yeast strain, temperature, and desired
flavor profile. Typically, fermentation can take
anywhere from a few days to a couple of weeks.
Monitor the progress by observing the activity
in the airlock and by taking gravity readings
using a hydrometer. Once the gravity stabilizes
and reaches the desired level, fermentation is
complete.

f) Hygiene and Sanitation: Throughout the
fermentation process, it is crucial to maintain a

clean and sanitary environment. This includes properly sanitizing all equipment, ensuring proper sealing of fermentation vessels, and practicing good hygiene when handling ingredients and working around the fermentation area. Any contamination can negatively impact the quality of your final product.

By paying attention to these key factors and practicing proper monitoring and control, you can optimize the fermentation process and achieve consistent and flavorful results.

Remember, patience is key during fermentation. Allow the yeast to work its magic, converting sugars into alcohol and developing complex flavors. Embrace the opportunity to experiment with different ingredients, yeast strains, and fermentation techniques to craft unique and personalized spirits.

CHAPTER 3. VODKA: FROM GRAIN TO BOTTLE

Understanding vodka production

Vodka, renowned for its clear and neutral taste, has become a beloved spirit enjoyed by people worldwide. Whether sipped neat, used as a base for cocktails, or infused with flavors, vodka holds a special place in the hearts of spirits enthusiasts. In this chapter, we will delve into the art and science of vodka production, providing you with a comprehensive understanding of the process from grain to bottle. Vodka, at its core, is a distilled spirit made through the fermentation and distillation of various agricultural materials. The word "vodka" is derived from the Slavic word "voda," meaning water, reflecting its long-standing association with purity and clarity.

The primary ingredients used in vodka production are water and a source of fermentable sugars. Traditionally, vodka has been made from grains such as wheat, rye, or barley. However, modern vodka production also encompasses the use of other agricultural products like potatoes, corn, and even grapes.

Distillation is a crucial process in the production of vodka, playing a central role in transforming a fermented mixture into a pure and high-quality spirit. This chapter will delve into the intricacies of distillation and explore its indispensable role in creating exceptional vodka. We will unravel the science behind distillation, examine the equipment involved, and gain an understanding of the various steps that make up this fascinating process. At its core, distillation is the art of separating alcohol from other substances through evaporation and condensation. This process allows the distiller to concentrate the alcohol content and eliminate unwanted impurities, resulting in a smoother and purer spirit. In the case of vodka, distillation is paramount in achieving the distinctive neutrality and crispness that define this beloved beverage.

To carry out the distillation process effectively, a well-designed set of equipment is required. A typical distillation setup for vodka production includes a still, which consists of a boiler, a column, and a condenser. The boiler heats the fermented mixture, while the column provides a means for the vapors to rise and condense. Finally, the condenser cools the vapors, transforming them back into a liquid state.

Step-by-Step Guide to the Distillation Process

A. Preparation and Fermentation of the Base Ingredients

Before distillation can begin, the base ingredients for vodka production must be carefully prepared and fermented. Commonly, grains such as wheat, rye, or corn are used, along with water and enzymes, to convert starches into fermentable sugars. The resulting mixture, known as the wash, is then ready for distillation.

B. Mashing and Converting Starches into Sugars

To extract the fermentable sugars from the grains, a process called mashing takes place. This involves grinding the grains and combining them with warm water, creating an environment that facilitates the conversion of starches into sugars. Enzymes, such as amylase, aid in this transformation, breaking down the complex carbohydrates into simpler sugars that yeast can ferment.

C. Fermentation and the Role of Yeast

Once the mash is prepared, it undergoes fermentation. Yeast, a microorganism, is introduced to the mash, converting the sugars into alcohol and carbon dioxide through a natural metabolic process known as fermentation. This results in the formation of a low-alcohol liquid called the wash, which serves as the starting point for distillation.

D. Distillation and Separation of Alcohol from Impurities

The heart of the distillation process begins with heating the wash in the still's boiler. As the temperature rises, alcohol vapors are released and ascend through the column. The column contains plates or packing material that allow the vapors to interact with cooler surfaces, encouraging condensation. This separation process is essential for eliminating impurities, as substances with higher boiling points remain in the still while the alcohol vapors rise towards the condenser.

E. Collecting and Controlling the Distillate

Once the alcohol vapors reach the condenser, they are cooled and converted back into liquid form. This resulting liquid, known as the distillate or "new make" spirit, contains a higher concentration of alcohol compared to the original wash. However, it is still not ready to be considered vodka.

Collecting the distillate requires careful attention and skill. The distiller must discard the initial and final portions of the distillate, known as the "heads" and "tails," respectively. The heads contain volatile compounds and higher alcohols that can impart unpleasant flavors and aromas. On the other hand, the tails consist of heavier compounds that can contribute to a harsh and oily texture. The goal is to isolate the "heart" or "middle cut" of the distillate, which contains the purest and most desirable flavors and aromas. This portion typically corresponds to a specific range of alcohol content, determined by the distiller's expertise and the desired characteristics of the vodka. Careful control over the temperature and flow rate during distillation helps achieve this separation.

To ensure consistency and quality, many distillers opt for multiple distillations or additional refining processes. Double or triple distillation can further purify the spirit, enhancing its smoothness and removing any remaining impurities. Each distillation round allows for a finer level of control over the flavor profile and ensures a cleaner final product.

Recipes and Techniques for Grain-based Vodka

Crafting your own grain-based vodka at home allows for experimentation with flavors and the opportunity to create a spirit tailored to your preferences. Here are some recipes and techniques to get you started:

Traditional Grain Vodka:

Ingredients:

- 4 pounds (1.8 kg) of high-quality grain (wheat, rye, or barley)
- 5 gallons (19 liters) of water
- Distillers yeast

Procedure:

a. Mash the grains by grinding them into a coarse meal.
b. Mix the mashed grains with water, creating a mash with the consistency of porridge.
c. Heat the mash to a temperature of 150°F (65°C) and maintain it for about 1 hour.
d. Allow the mash to cool to room temperature, then add the distiller's yeast.
e. Ferment the mash in a sealed container for approximately 5-7 days or until fermentation ceases.
f. Distill the fermented wash using a pot still or reflux still, collecting the middle cut or heart of the distillate.
g. Dilute the distillate to your desired proof using distilled water.

Infusing Vodka with Flavors

One of the joys of vodka production is the ability to infuse the spirit with various flavors, allowing for a personal touch and unique creations. Here are some popular flavor infusion techniques to explore:

- **Fruit Infusions:**

Fruit-infused vodkas add a delightful burst of natural flavors. To create fruit-infused vodka, select your favorite fruits such as berries, citrus fruits, or tropical delights like pineapple or mango. Wash and cut the fruits, then place them in a clean glass jar. Pour vodka over the fruits, ensuring they are fully submerged. Seal the jar and let it sit for a week or two, allowing the flavors to meld. You can adjust the infusion time based on your desired intensity of flavor. Once infused, strain the vodka to remove the fruit pieces, and you're left with a vibrant and fruity vodka ready to be enjoyed.

- **Herb and Spice Infusions:**

Experimenting with herbs and spices can yield intriguing and aromatic vodka infusions. Popular choices include vanilla beans, cinnamon sticks, fresh herbs like rosemary or thyme, or exotic spices like cardamom or star anise. Simply add your selected herbs or spices to a clean glass jar, pour vodka over them, and seal the jar. Allow the flavors to infuse for about a week, tasting periodically to achieve your desired intensity. Strain the vodka to remove the herbs or spices, and revel in the intriguing flavors of your homemade herb or spice-infused vodka.

- **Floral Infusions:**

For a touch of elegance, floral infusions offer a delicate and fragrant twist to vodka. Edible flowers such as lavender, rose petals, or hibiscus can infuse vodka with their enchanting aromas. Similar to fruit and herb infusions, place the chosen flowers in a glass jar, cover them with vodka, and seal the jar. Let the mixture sit for a week or more, allowing the vodka to capture the floral essence. Once the infusion is complete, strain the vodka to remove the flower petals, and behold the captivating floral notes in your homemade vodka.

Filtering and Bottling Vodka

After distillation and infusion, the final step in producing your own vodka at home involves filtering and bottling. Filtering helps remove any remaining impurities and ensures a smooth and pristine finish to your spirit. There are various filtration techniques you can employ to refine your vodka. One common method is using activated carbon or charcoal filters. Pour your vodka through a filter lined with activated carbon, allowing it to pass through slowly, capturing impurities along the way. Another technique is employing multiple filtrations passes using different filtration media such as paper filters, ceramic filters, or even specialized vodka filtration systems available in the market. Experiment with different filtration methods to find the one that suits your taste preferences.

Once your vodka is filtered to perfection, it's time to bottle it for storage and enjoyment. Use clean glass bottles with airtight seals to preserve the quality of your vodka. Consider adding personalized labels or decorative touches to your bottles, giving them a professional and stylish appearance. Remember to store your vodka in a cool, dark place away from direct sunlight to maintain its flavors and integrity. By understanding vodka production, exploring different recipes and infusions, and mastering filtration and bottling techniques, you can embark on an exciting journey of creating your own unique vodka at home. Enjoy the process, embrace creativity, and savor the fruits of your labor as you sip on a truly personalized spirit.

Remember, responsible consumption of alcohol is vital, and always ensure compliance with legal regulations and safety guidelines when engaging in home distilling activities.

The Importance of Distillation in Vodka Production

Distillation is the cornerstone of vodka production, playing a pivotal role in shaping the character and quality of the spirit. Here are a few key reasons why distillation is essential:

Purity and Neutrality: Distillation eliminates impurities and unwanted flavors, resulting in a clean and neutral base spirit. This neutrality serves as a canvas for further refinement and allows for the infusion of flavors or blending to create a wide variety of vodka styles.

Alcohol Concentration: Distillation enables the concentration of alcohol content in vodka. By removing water and other compounds with higher boiling points, the distiller can achieve the desired strength of the spirit, typically ranging from 40% to 50% alcohol by volume (ABV).

Flavor and Aroma Development: While vodka is known for its neutrality, the distillation process also contribute to subtle flavor and aroma characteristics. The choice of base ingredients, fermentation techniques, and the precise separation of the distillate all influence the final profile of the vodka, resulting in variations that can be appreciated by discerning consumers.

Distillation is the transformative process that elevates the fermented mixture to the pure and refined spirit we know as vodka. By harnessing the principles of evaporation and condensation, distillation allows distillers to create a spirit that embodies purity, neutrality, and distinctive flavors. Understanding the science behind distillation and mastering the art of collecting the heart cut are essential skills for any aspiring home distiller. With patience, precision, and a deep appreciation for the craft, you can embark on a journey to create your very own exceptional vodka.

CHAPTER FOUR - WHISKEY:
THE ART OF AGING AND FLAVOR

Whiskey, often regarded as the king of spirits, is a timeless alcoholic beverage with a rich history and a global following. Known for its complex flavors, distinct aromas, and diverse styles, whiskey is produced through a meticulous process that involves the careful selection of ingredients, fermentation, distillation, and maturation. Whether enjoyed neat, on the rocks, or in a classic cocktail, whiskey captivates connoisseurs and enthusiasts alike. In this introduction, we will explore the fascinating world of whiskey production, delving into its origins, the different types of whiskey, and the key steps involved in crafting this revered spirit.

Different Types of Whiskey

Whiskey is a diverse and captivating spirit with a wide range of styles and flavors that cater to various preferences. In this chapter, we will explore some of the most well-known types of whiskey, including Scotch, Irish, bourbon, and rye. Each variety possesses its own unique characteristics, production methods, and regional influences, making the world of whiskey a truly fascinating one to explore.

- **Scotch Whisky:**

Scotch whisky, often simply referred to as Scotch, holds a special place in the hearts of whiskey connoisseurs. It is made primarily from malted barley and distilled in Scotland. Scotch whiskies are renowned for their distinctive smoky and peaty flavors, which are derived from the traditional process of drying malted barley over a peat fire. There are two main categories of Scotch whisky: single malt and blended. Single malt Scotch whisky is made from malted barley and distilled at a single distillery, while blended Scotch whisky combines malt whiskies from different distilleries with grain whisky.

- **Irish Whiskey:**

Irish whiskey has a long and storied history, known for its smoothness and approachability. It is typically made from a mixture of malted and unmalted barley, which undergoes triple distillation. The triple distillation process contributes to Irish whiskey's lighter and smoother character. Unlike Scotch whisky, Irish whiskey does not use peat during the malting process, resulting in a cleaner and less smoky flavor profile. Irish whiskey is appreciated for its versatility, making it suitable for sipping neat, mixing in cocktails, or enjoying with a dash of water.

- **Bourbon Whiskey:**

Bourbon is a distinctly American whiskey and holds a special place in American culture. To be classified as bourbon, it must be made primarily from corn (at least 51% corn), distilled at no more than 160 proof, and aged in new charred oak barrels. Bourbon often showcases a sweet and rich flavor profile with notes of caramel, vanilla, and oak. While it can be produced anywhere in the United States, it is most closely associated with the state of Kentucky. The limestone-rich water in Kentucky is believed to contribute to the quality and character of the bourbon produced in the region.

- **Rye Whiskey:**

Rye whiskey is known for its bold and spicy character, making it a favorite among whiskey enthusiasts seeking a robust flavor profile. It is made primarily from rye grain and can contain a small percentage of malted barley and corn. Rye whiskey offers a distinct and assertive taste, with flavors ranging from peppery spice to fruity and floral notes. Like bourbon, rye whiskey must be aged in new charred oak barrels, although it doesn't have a specific geographic association like bourbon does.

It is worth noting that these four types of whiskey represent just a fraction of the diverse whiskey landscape. Other notable varieties include Tennessee whiskey (similar to bourbon but with an additional charcoal filtration process known as the Lincoln County Process) and Canadian whisky (often made from a blend of grains and aged in oak barrels). Additionally, various countries around the world, such as Japan and Australia, have started producing their own unique styles of whiskey, adding even more variety and complexity to the global whiskey scene.

Exploring the different types of whiskey allows enthusiasts to develop their palates, appreciate various flavor profiles, and discover their personal preferences. Each type of whiskey has its own distinctive charm and allure, reflecting the traditions, craftsmanship, and terroir of its origin. As we continue our journey into home distilling, understanding these whiskey styles will provide a solid foundation for crafting your own unique spirits. In the next chapter, we will dive into the crucial step of mash preparation, where the flavors and character of whiskey truly begin to take shape.

Mash Preparation

The mash is a crucial component in the whiskey-making process, playing a pivotal role in flavor development and alcohol production. It serves as the foundation for the fermentation stage, where the conversion of grains into sugars occurs. Understanding the significance of the mash and its intricacies is essential for aspiring home distillers seeking to create high-quality whiskey.

The mash is essentially a mixture of grains and water that undergoes enzymatic activity to convert starches into fermentable sugars. The choice of grains and their proportions can significantly influence the flavor profile of the final product. Common grains used in whiskey production include barley, corn, rye, and wheat, each offering distinct flavors and characteristics.

During the mashing process, the grains are finely ground to expose a larger surface area, allowing enzymes to efficiently convert starches into sugars. Water is added to the grains, and the mixture is gradually heated in a vessel known as a mash tun. This heating process activates the enzymes present in the malted grains, primarily amylase and glucanase, which break down the complex starches into simpler sugars.

The two primary types of amylase enzymes involved in the mash are alpha-amylase and beta-amylase. Alpha-amylase works at higher temperatures, breaking down the starches into longer chains of sugars, including maltose and dextrins. Beta-amylase functions at lower temperatures, further breaking down the long chains into simpler sugars like glucose. The interaction between these enzymes and the temperature conditions during mashing greatly influences the sugar composition and fermentability of the resulting wort.

Step-by-Step Guide for Creating the Mash

Creating a well-crafted mash requires careful attention to detail and precision. Follow these step-by-step guidelines to achieve optimal results:

- **Grain Selection**: Choose the grains based on the desired flavor profile and whiskey style you intend to produce. Consider the proportions of each grain, as they will impact the overall character of the mash.
- **Milling**: Grind the grains to a consistent and fine texture. This increases the surface area and enhances enzyme accessibility during mashing. Aim for a coarseness that allows for efficient starch conversion without producing excessive amounts of husk material that could lead to filtration issues.
- **Water-to-Grain Ratio**: Calculate the appropriate water-to-grain ratio based on the specific grains and desired thickness of the mash. Typically, a ratio of around 1.5 to 3 liters of water per kilogram of grain is suitable, but adjustments may be needed based on the grains used and personal preference.
- **Mashing-in**: Add the milled grains to the mash tun, and slowly mix in hot water at a

specific temperature range. The temperature depends on the desired enzyme activity and sugar composition. For example, a temperature of around 63-68°C (145-155°F) promotes beta-amylase activity, favoring the production of fermentable sugars.

- **Saccharification Rest**: Maintain the mash temperature within the desired range for a specific duration, typically around 60 to 90 minutes. This allows the enzymes to convert the starches into fermentable sugars. Stir occasionally to ensure even heat distribution and enzyme contact with the grains.

- **Mash-out**: Raise the mash temperature to denature the enzymes and halt further enzymatic activity. This step ensures the desired sugar composition is achieved without continued starch conversion. Heating the mash to approximately 75-78°C (167-172°F) for a short period, around 10-15 minutes, is sufficient for mash-out.

- **Lautering**: After the mash-out, separate the liquid portion (wort) from the spent grains in a process called lautering. Lautering involves transferring the mash to a separate vessel or using a straining mechanism to separate the liquid wort from the solid grain particles. This step ensures a clear and clean wort, ready for fermentation.

- **Sparging**: Rinse the spent grains with hot water to extract any remaining sugars from the grain bed. This process, known as sparging, helps maximize the sugar yield and efficiency of the mash. The sparge water is typically heated to a temperature near the mash temperature to maintain consistency.

- **Wort Collection**: Collect the wort in a separate container, ready for fermentation. It is important to handle the wort carefully, avoiding excessive agitation or the introduction of contaminants that could affect the quality of the final whiskey.

By following these steps, you will have successfully created a mash ready for fermentation. The mash serves as the starting point for the transformation of grains into alcohol, setting the stage for the next crucial stage in whiskey production.

In the next section, we will explore the art of fermentation, discussing its role in converting the sugars in the mash into alcohol and the factors that influence this transformative process. Understanding fermentation is essential for aspiring home distillers to produce flavorful and high-quality whiskey. So let's delve into the fascinating world of fermentation in our whiskey-making journey.

Fermentation-The Role of Fermentation in the Whiskey-Making Process

Fermentation is a pivotal step in the whiskey-making process, where the sugars present in the mash are transformed into alcohol. This transformative stage involves the introduction of yeast, which consumes sugars and produces alcohol and carbon dioxide as byproducts. Understanding the role of fermentation and the factors that influence this process is crucial for producing flavorful and well-rounded whiskey.

Fermentation serves two primary purposes in whiskey production. Firstly, it converts the sugars derived from the grains during mashing into alcohol, which is essential for creating the desired alcoholic content of the whiskey. Secondly, fermentation contributes to the development of unique flavors and aromas, as yeast interacts with the other components present in the mash.

Detailed Instructions on Fermenting the Mash

Achieving successful fermentation requires careful attention to key factors such as temperature control, yeast selection, and fermentation duration. Follow these step-by-step guidelines to ensure a smooth and effective fermentation process:

- **Yeast Selection:** Choose a suitable yeast strain that complements the desired flavor profile of the whiskey. Different yeast strains can produce distinct flavors and aromas during fermentation. Common yeast options for whiskey production include Saccharomyces cerevisiae and various distiller yeast strains specifically formulated for whiskey.
- **Pitching the Yeast:** Once the mash has been prepared and cooled to an appropriate temperature range, typically around 21-32°C (70-90°F), it is ready for yeast inoculation. Add the yeast to the mash, ensuring it is evenly distributed. The yeast will begin consuming the sugars and converting them into alcohol.
- **Temperature Control:** Maintain consistent and controlled temperatures throughout the fermentation process. The optimal temperature

range for whiskey fermentation depends on the yeast strain used, but it generally falls within 21-32°C (70-90°F). Yeast activity and flavor development can vary significantly with temperature, so it is crucial to monitor and control the fermentation environment.

- **Fermentation Vessel:** Transfer the yeast-inoculated mash into a suitable fermentation vessel, such as a fermentation barrel or a food-grade plastic or stainless-steel container. Ensure the vessel is properly sanitized to prevent contamination and unwanted off-flavors.
- **Fermentation Duration:** The fermentation duration can vary depending on several factors, including yeast strain, temperature, and desired flavor profile. Typically, fermentation for whiskey ranges from several days to a week or longer. Monitor the fermentation progress by observing the activity of the yeast (such as the formation of bubbles and foam) and by periodically testing the specific gravity of the liquid using a hydrometer.
- **Hygiene and Contamination Prevention:** Maintain a clean and sanitary environment throughout the fermentation process to prevent the growth of unwanted bacteria or wild yeast strains. Proper sanitation practices, such as sanitizing equipment and ensuring the vessel is sealed to prevent air exposure, are essential to producing high-quality whiskey.
- **Monitoring Fermentation:** Regularly monitor the fermentation progress, paying attention to factors such as yeast activity,

temperature, and specific gravity. These indicators can help ensure a successful fermentation and allow you to make any necessary adjustments if needed.

- **Completion of Fermentation:** Fermentation is considered complete when the yeast has converted most of the sugars into alcohol, and the specific gravity stabilizes. This can typically be determined when the specific gravity reading remains consistent over consecutive days.

By following these guidelines, you can ensure a successful fermentation process that yields a flavorful and well-fermented wash ready for distillation. Fermentation is a critical stage in whiskey production, as it sets the foundation for the final flavors and character of the whiskey.

Aging and Maturation

Aging is a transformative process that gives whiskey its complexity, depth, and character. Whiskey spends time maturing in barrels, allowing it to interact with the wood and undergo chemical reactions that shape its flavor profile. In this chapter, we will delve into the significance of aging and explore various methods for aging whiskey at home.

Aging whiskey is a crucial step in the production process, as it allows the spirit to mature and develop unique flavors and aromas. During aging, whiskey undergoes a series of complex interactions with the wood of the barrel, leading to the extraction of compounds such as tannins, lignins, and vanillin. These compounds contribute to the development of flavors like vanilla, caramel, and spice, enhancing the overall complexity of the whiskey.

Additionally, aging allows for the oxidation of the whiskey, which can mellow harsh flavors and create a smoother and more refined drinking experience. The interaction with oxygen also enables the integration and harmonization of various components, resulting in a well-balanced and nuanced whiskey.

Various Methods for Aging Whiskey at Home

Aging whiskey at home can be a rewarding and exciting process, allowing you to customize the maturation of your spirits. While traditional aging typically takes place in oak barrels, there are alternative methods that can be employed on a smaller scale. Here are some methods you can explore:

- **Oak Barrels**: The most authentic and traditional method of aging whiskey is the use of oak barrels. Oak provides a porous structure that allows the whiskey to breathe and interact with the wood's compounds. If you choose to age your whiskey in oak barrels, ensure they are specifically designed for spirits and have been properly charred or toasted to enhance flavor extraction.
- **Oak Chips or Staves**: For those who prefer a smaller-scale approach, oak chips or staves can be used to mimic the effects of aging in barrels. These wooden pieces can be added directly to the whiskey, providing similar flavor-enhancing characteristics. Experiment with different types of oak (such as American,

French, or Hungarian) and levels of toasting to achieve desired flavor profiles.

- **Toasted Wood Spirals:** Wood spirals offer another option for aging whiskey at home. These spiral-shaped wooden inserts can be added to the whiskey, allowing for increased surface area contact and flavor extraction. Like oak chips or staves, they come in various toasting levels and wood types, providing flexibility in flavor experimentation.
- **Aging in Glass Containers:** Aging whiskey in glass containers, such as mason jars or demijohns, can be an alternative method for those seeking a different aging experience. While glass does not impart flavors like wood does, it still allows the whiskey to undergo oxidation and develop subtle changes over time.

Tips for Monitoring and Maintaining the Aging Process

When aging whiskey at home, it is crucial to monitor and maintain the aging process to achieve desired results. Here are some tips to consider:

- Time and Patience: Aging whiskey takes time, and it's essential to be patient throughout the process. The duration of aging can vary based on personal preference and the desired flavor profile. Regularly taste your whiskey to track its progress and adjust aging time accordingly.
- Storage Conditions: Proper storage conditions are important for aging whiskey. Keep the aging containers in a cool, dark place with

stable temperatures to avoid excessive fluctuations that could impact the maturation process. Aim for a temperature range of around 15-20°C (59-68°F).

- Sampling and Evaluation: Regularly sample and evaluate the whiskey during the aging process. Take note of the changes in aroma, color, and taste over time to assess the whiskey's development. This allows you to understand how the flavors are evolving and make any necessary adjustments or decisions regarding the aging duration.

- Seal Integrity: Ensure that the aging containers are properly sealed to prevent excessive evaporation and maintain a consistent aging environment. Check for any leaks or gaps that could compromise the aging process.

- Dilution and Proofing: As whiskey ages, it may undergo concentration due to evaporation. Monitor the whiskey's proof (alcohol content) and consider diluting it with distilled water if necessary to maintain the desired strength. Keep in mind that dilution can also affect the flavor profile, so adjust carefully.

- Note Taking: Maintain a detailed record of your aging process, including dates, types of wood used, toasting levels, and any other relevant information. This allows you to track the progression of different batches and helps you replicate successful outcomes in the future.

Remember, aging is a subjective process, and experimentation is key to finding the flavor profile that suits your preferences. Embrace the journey of aging your own whiskey and enjoy the anticipation of tasting the final product.

Quality Assessment

Assessing the quality of homemade whiskey is an essential skill for any aspiring distiller. By employing various techniques, you can evaluate the aroma, taste, and overall character of your whiskey, allowing you to refine your craft and create exceptional spirits. In this chapter, we will explore different methods of quality assessment to help you develop a discerning palate and produce high-quality whiskey.

Aroma Evaluation:

- Pour a small amount of whiskey into a tulip-shaped glass and swirl it gently to release the aromas.
- Place your nose above the glass and take a slow, deep breath to capture the fragrance.
- Analyze the aroma for different scent profiles such as fruity, floral, spicy, woody, or caramel notes.
- Note the intensity, complexity, and balance of the aromas.

Appearance Assessment:

- Observe the color and clarity of the whiskey. Hold the glass against a white background to better evaluate the hue.
- Note the intensity, richness, and consistency of the color. Whiskey can range from pale straw to deep amber, depending on factors like aging and cask type.

Taste Analysis:

- Take a small sip of whiskey and let it coat your entire palate. Allow the flavors to develop and linger.
- Evaluate the taste for characteristics like sweetness, bitterness, spiciness, and complexity.
- Note the balance of flavors, the mouthfeel (viscosity and texture), and the length of the finish (how long the flavors persist after swallowing).

Flavor Profiling:

- Pay attention to specific flavor components such as fruitiness (citrus, orchard fruits, tropical fruits), sweetness (caramel, honey, vanilla), spiciness (cinnamon, clove, pepper), and wood influence (oak, smoke, char).
- Analyze the interplay and intensity of these flavors, identifying any dominant or subtle notes.
- Consider how the flavors evolve throughout the tasting experience.

Comparative Tasting:

- Conduct side-by-side tastings of different whiskey samples to compare and contrast their qualities.

- Assess the similarities and differences in aroma, taste, and overall character.
- Look for nuances that set each whiskey apart and identify personal preferences.

Factors to Consider when Assessing Aroma, Taste, and Overall Character

When evaluating the quality of homemade whiskey, several factors come into play. Here are some key considerations to keep in mind during the assessment process:

- Balance: A well-balanced whiskey exhibits harmony between its various components, including aroma, taste, and finish. No single element should overpower the others.
- Complexity: Complexity refers to the presence of multiple layers of aroma and flavor. Look for a whiskey that offers depth and nuance, with different notes revealing themselves over time.
- Smoothness: Smoothness refers to the absence of harsh or abrasive flavors and a pleasant mouthfeel. A smooth whiskey will glide across the palate without any rough edges.
- Distinctiveness: Consider whether the whiskey has unique qualities that set it apart from others. Look for distinct flavor profiles, uncommon aromas, or a particular character that makes it memorable.
- Consistency: Evaluate the consistency of your whiskey across multiple batches. Aim for a consistent flavor profile and quality, indicating your ability to reproduce successful results.

- Maturity: Aging plays a significant role in the maturity of whiskey. Consider whether the flavors and aromas have developed and integrated well over time, resulting in a refined and matured spirit.
- Personal Preference: Ultimately, the assessment of whiskey quality is subjective. Consider your personal preferences and whether the whiskey aligns with your desired flavor profile. It's important to trust your own taste buds and evaluate the whiskey-based on your individual preferences and expectations.
- Consideration of Style: When assessing the quality of whiskey, take into account the specific style or category it belongs to. Different styles, such as Scotch, Irish, bourbon, or rye, have distinct flavor profiles and characteristics. Evaluate the whiskey-based on how well it represents and adheres to the characteristics of its respective style.
- Aging and Maturation: Consider the impact of aging and maturation on the whiskey's quality. A well-aged whiskey often exhibits greater complexity and depth of flavor compared to a younger spirit. Evaluate how the aging process has contributed to the overall character of the whiskey.
- Feedback and Collaboration: Seek feedback from others, such as fellow whiskey enthusiasts or experienced distillers, to gain different perspectives on the quality of your whiskey. Engaging in tasting sessions and discussions

with others can provide valuable insights and help you refine your assessment skills.

Remember, quality assessment is a continuous learning process. The more you practice, the better you will become at discerning the nuances and characteristics of whiskey. As you refine your evaluation skills, you will gain a deeper appreciation for the craftsmanship and artistry involved in producing exceptional spirits.

Safety and Responsible Consumption

While the art of home distilling allows you to create your own spirits and explore the world of flavors, it is essential to prioritize safety and responsible consumption. Understanding the potential risks associated with alcohol production and consumption can help you enjoy your homemade spirits in a responsible and enjoyable manner. So, grab your glass (of water), and let's dive into the serious side of distilling with a touch of humor.

- **Safety First:** Just like wearing oven mitts when handling hot pans, safety should always be your priority when distilling. Familiarize yourself with safety procedures, such as proper equipment handling, ventilation, and fire safety. Remember, you want your spirits to be fiery, not your distilling equipment!
- The Proof is in Moderation: It's important to approach alcohol consumption with moderation. Enjoying your homemade spirits in moderation not only ensures your well-being but also allows you to fully appreciate the flavors and craftsmanship behind your

creations. Remember, too much of a good thing can lead to a "spirited" adventure you might not remember!

- **Educate and Inform:** Share your knowledge with friends and fellow enthusiasts to promote responsible alcohol consumption. Educate them about the importance of understanding alcohol content, pacing themselves, and knowing their limits. Be the whiskey guru who spreads wisdom and good cheer!

Potential Risks and Legal Implications of Improper Distillation

While distilling at home can be an exciting and rewarding hobby, it's crucial to be aware of the potential risks and legal implications that can arise from improper practices. Let's explore these with a light-hearted touch to keep the mood balanced.

- The "Still" ness of Danger: Improper distillation techniques can pose risks such as fire hazards, explosions, or the production of harmful substances. Remember, you want your spirits to ignite passion, not your distillery!
- Uncle Sam's Watchful Eye: Familiarize yourself with the legal regulations and restrictions surrounding home distilling in your area. Distilling in accordance with the law ensures you stay on the right side of the whiskey angels and avoid any legal entanglements. Don't let your distilling hobby become a "distilled" nightmare!
- Responsible Hosting: If you plan on sharing your homemade spirits with friends or hosting

tastings, it's important to ensure that everyone drinks responsibly. Provide non-alcoholic alternatives, encourage designated drivers, and create an atmosphere that promotes enjoyment without excess. Remember, a good host knows how to keep the party spirited but safe!

- By incorporating safety practices and promoting responsible consumption, you can enjoy the fruits of your distilling labor while maintaining a fun and safe environment. So, raise your glass (filled with water, of course) to the responsible distiller who knows how to keep it safe and enjoyable!

Congratulations! You have now journeyed through the world of home distilling, from the overview of whiskey production to the techniques of quality assessment and the importance of responsible consumption. Armed with this knowledge and a pinch of humor, you are well-equipped to embark on your own distilling adventures.

Remember, distilling is an art form that requires passion, patience, and attention to detail. Take pride in your creations, experiment with flavors, and continue to refine your skills. Share the joy of homemade spirits with friends and loved ones, always keeping in mind the importance of responsible consumption.

As you raise your glass and savor the flavors, may you find fulfillment in the craft of distilling and the delightful moments it brings. Cheers to your whiskey-making journey, filled with laughter, good company, and a taste of your own liquid alchemy!

CHAPTER 5-DISTILLING FRUITS INTO ELEGANCE

Brandy, derived from the Dutch word "brandewijn," meaning "burnt wine," has a rich history that dates back centuries. Its origins can be traced to the development of distillation techniques in the Mediterranean region during the Middle Ages. Brandy gained popularity as a way to preserve wine and facilitate transportation during long sea voyages. In addition to its practical uses, brandy became a symbol of status and sophistication. It was favored by aristocrats and nobility, who appreciated its smoothness, depth of flavor, and ability to age gracefully. Brandy also played a significant role in religious and cultural ceremonies, making it an integral part of many traditions around the world.

Brandy exudes an aura of elegance and sophistication that sets it apart from other spirits. Its golden hues, complex aromas, and refined taste make it a favorite among discerning palates. Brandy's versatility allows it to be enjoyed on its own, as a digestif, or as a key ingredient in various cocktails. Connoisseurs and enthusiasts appreciate the craftsmanship and artistry that goes into producing exceptional brandy. The meticulous selection of fruits, careful fermentation, precise distillation, and patient aging all contribute to its allure. Each bottle of brandy tells a unique story, reflecting the expertise of the distiller and the distinctive characteristics of the fruit from which it is made.

Over time, brandy-making techniques have evolved, leading to advancements in production methods and the refinement of flavors. Early brandy production involved simple pot stills, which gradually evolved into more sophisticated distillation apparatuses such as column stills and continuous stills.

The introduction of aging in oak barrels was a turning point in brandy production, as it allowed for the development of intricate flavor profiles and the integration of wood-derived compounds. Additionally, innovations in distillation equipment and temperature control techniques have enabled distillers to achieve greater consistency and precision in their products. The knowledge and experience passed down through generations, coupled with technological advancements, have contributed to the improvement and diversification of brandy production methods. Today, a balance between tradition and innovation ensures the continuation of Brandy's legacy as a revered spirit.

Distillation and how they are applied in brandy production.

Distillation, the process at the heart of brandy production, involves separating alcohol from fermented liquids by exploiting differences in boiling points. This method allows for the concentration of alcohol and the removal of impurities. The distillation process begins by heating the fermented liquid, typically wine, in a still. As the liquid heats up, the alcohol evaporates at a lower temperature than water, rising as vapor. The vapor is then captured and cooled, causing it to condense back into a liquid form. This condensed liquid, known as distillate, contains a higher concentration of alcohol. In brandy production, the distillation process is often performed in multiple stages to achieve a desired level of purity and flavor refinement. Single distillation involves a single pass through the still, while double distillation includes a second distillation of the initial distillate.

During distillation, the process is divided into three distinct fractions: the "heads," the "hearts," and the "tails." The heads fraction consists of volatile compounds with strong and unpleasant flavors, while the hearts fraction contains the desired aromatic and flavorful components. The tails fraction consists of heavier compounds and impurities.

To produce high-quality brandy, it is crucial to separate these fractions carefully. The heads and tails are usually discarded or recycled for further distillation, while the hearts fraction is collected and used to create the brandy. This careful separation ensures that only the most desirable flavors and aromas are retained, resulting in a refined and balanced spirit. The fundamental principles of distillation are essential in brandy production, as they determine the character and quality of the final product. Master distillers rely on their expertise to make precise cuts during the distillation process, capturing the essence of the fruit and creating brandies with distinct flavor profiles.

By understanding the historical significance, cultural importance, and evolution of brandy-making techniques, as well as the fundamental principles of distillation, enthusiasts can develop a deeper appreciation for this exquisite spirit. With this knowledge as a foundation, we can now explore the next step in brandy production: fruit selection and fermentation.

Fruit Selection and Fermentation

In brandy production, the selection of fruits is a critical factor that significantly influences the final flavor and aroma of the spirit. Different fruits lend their unique characteristics to the brandy, resulting in a diverse range of styles and profiles.

Grapes are the most commonly used fruit for brandy production, particularly in renowned varieties such as Cognac and Armagnac. The specific grape varieties chosen, such as Ugni Blanc, Folle Blanche, or Colombard, contribute to the flavor, acidity, and sugar content of the brandy.

Apples are another popular fruit used in brandy production, especially in regions known for their apple brandies. Varieties like the Calvados apples in Normandy, France, or the American apple brandies made from specific apple cultivars, offer distinct flavors ranging from crisp and tart to rich and fruity.

Pears have their own place in brandy production, as they provide a delicate and aromatic character to the spirit. Poire Williams, made from the Williams pear, is a notable example of pear brandy that captures the fruit's unique essence.

Cherries, such as the Marasca variety, are used to produce cherry brandies like Kirsch. These brandies often exhibit a vibrant cherry flavor and are valued for their use in cocktails and culinary applications.

The choice of fruit is crucial in brandy production, as it sets the foundation for the spirit's flavor and aroma. Each fruit imparts its own distinct qualities, making the selection process an essential step in creating a remarkable brandy.

After selecting the desired fruit, the fermentation process plays a vital role in transforming the fruit sugars into alcohol, laying the groundwork for brandy production.

Fermentation begins by crushing or pressing the fruit to extract its juice, which contains natural sugars. Yeast is then introduced to the juice, initiating the fermentation process. The yeast consumes the sugars and converts them into alcohol, releasing carbon dioxide as a byproduct. This conversion process, known as alcoholic fermentation, typically takes several days to complete. During fermentation, the temperature and environment are carefully controlled to ensure optimal yeast activity. The yeast strain used can also influence the flavors and aromas produced during fermentation, adding another layer of complexity to the brandy's profile.

The duration of fermentation varies depending on the desired characteristics of the brandy. Shorter fermentation times generally result in a fresher, fruitier spirit, while longer fermentations can develop more complex and nuanced flavors.

Fermentation is a critical step in brandy production as it sets the stage for distillation. The resulting fermented liquid, often referred to as "wine" in the context of brandy production, contains alcohol and a range of fruity flavors and aromas derived from the chosen fruit. This liquid is then distilled to concentrate the alcohol and capture the essence of the fruit, shaping the distinctive character of the brandy.

Distilling Techniques

In brandy production, different distillation techniques are employed to refine the fermented liquid and create a spirit of exceptional quality. The two primary techniques used are single distillation and double distillation.

Single Distillation: Single distillation involves passing the fermented liquid through a still once. This method is often employed in the production of fruit brandies, where the emphasis is on capturing the pure fruit essence. Single distillation can result in a spirit with a rich and pronounced fruit character, as fewer impurities are removed during the process.

Double Distillation: Double distillation, on the other hand, is a more complex and time-consuming method. It involves two separate distillation processes, resulting in a cleaner and more refined spirit. The first distillation, known as the "stripping run," aims to separate alcohol from impurities and unwanted compounds. The resulting distillate, known as "low wines," undergoes a second distillation, called the "spirit run," which further refines the spirit by removing undesirable elements and concentrating desirable flavors.

Double distillation is commonly employed in the production of Cognac and Armagnac, where the goal is to create a spirit with heightened elegance, depth, and complexity. This method allows distillers to carefully select and separate the different fractions of the distillate, including the heads, hearts, and tails, to achieve a refined and well-balanced brandy. During the distillation process, the fermented liquid is separated into three fractions: the heads, the hearts, and the tails. Each fraction contributes distinct elements to the flavor profile and quality of the brandy.

Heads: The heads fraction consists of volatile compounds that have lower boiling points than alcohol. These compounds, such as acetone and methanol, can have harsh and unpleasant flavors. To ensure a smooth and palatable brandy, the heads fraction is typically discarded or recycled for further distillation. Removing the heads fraction is crucial for producing high-quality brandy with a refined flavor profile.

Hearts: The heart's fraction, also known as the "middle cut," is the most desired portion of the distillate. It contains the desired aromatic compounds, flavors, and the majority of the alcohol content. The heart's fraction contributes to the character, complexity, and smoothness of the brandy. Distillers carefully monitor the temperature and vapor during distillation to separate and collect the hearts, ensuring that the spirit captures the essence of the fruit and exhibits the desired characteristics.

Tails: The tails fraction consists of heavier compounds with higher boiling points than alcohol. These compounds include fusel oils and fatty acids, which can impart undesirable flavors such as oily or greasy notes. The tails fraction is usually discarded or recycled, as it can detract from the overall quality of the brandy. Careful separation of the tails fraction helps maintain the purity and refinement of the final spirit.

By skillfully managing the heads, hearts, and tails fractions, distillers can control the flavor profile, balance, and overall quality of the brandy. This meticulous approach ensures that the brandy captures the essence of the fruit, offering a harmonious and enjoyable drinking experience.

Aging and Maturation

Aging plays a pivotal role in the production of brandy, transforming it from a raw distillate into a refined and sophisticated spirit. During the aging process, brandy undergoes a remarkable metamorphosis as it interacts with oak barrels, allowing for flavor development, complexity, and smoothness. One of the key elements in brandy aging is the use of oak barrels. These barrels provide a porous environment that allows the brandy to breathe and interact with the wood, imparting unique characteristics to the spirit. Oak contributes flavors such as vanilla, caramel, spice, and subtle hints of toast or smoke, adding depth and richness to the brandy's profile.

- Several factors influence the aging process of brandy, resulting in distinct characteristics and nuances:
- Climate: The climate in which brandy is aged significantly impacts the maturation process. In regions with a warmer climate, such as Cognac or Armagnac in France, the brandy interacts more intensely with the oak barrels

due to higher temperatures. This accelerated aging can result in a more pronounced extraction of flavors from the wood. In contrast, cooler climates may lead to slower maturation, allowing for a more delicate and gradual development of flavors.

- Storage Conditions: The storage conditions in which brandy is aged are crucial. Factors such as temperature, humidity, and air quality can affect the aging process. Controlled environments are often preferred, as they provide consistent conditions that allow the brandy to mature gracefully. Fluctuations in temperature and humidity can cause the expansion and contraction of the liquid, facilitating the extraction of flavors from the wood.
- Interaction with Wood: The interaction between the brandy and the oak barrels is a complex and dynamic process. As the brandy ages, it absorbs compounds from the wood, including tannins, lignins, and vanillin. These interactions contribute to the development of flavors, texture, and color in the brandy. Additionally, the porous nature of oak allows for gradual oxidation, which can soften harsh elements and enhance the overall balance of the spirit.

The careful management of these factors is essential in producing a well-aged brandy. Distillers and cellar masters rely on their expertise to select the appropriate barrels, monitor the aging environment, and determine the optimal aging period to achieve the desired flavor profile and quality in the brandy. By embracing the art of aging, brandy producers create spirits of extraordinary elegance and depth, inviting enthusiasts to embark on a sensory journey with every sip.

Blending and Artistry

Blending is a true art form in the world of brandy production. It is the meticulous process of combining different distillates, ages, and flavor profiles to achieve a final product that is greater than the sum of its parts. Blending requires a deep understanding of the individual characteristics of each distillate and the ability to balance them harmoniously. The art of blending begins with the selection of various distillates. Each distillate, obtained through the distillation process, possesses unique qualities, such as fruitiness, depth, or complexity. Blenders carefully assess these distillates, keeping in mind their desired flavor profile, and experiment with different combinations to achieve the desired result.

Blenders employ their sensory expertise to evaluate and assess each distillate's aroma, flavor, and texture. They identify the strengths and weaknesses of each component, understanding how they can complement or enhance one another. This delicate balancing act requires a keen palate, experience, and intuition to create a brandy that embodies complexity, smoothness, and character. Furthermore, blenders consider the aging expressions available to them. Different age expressions bring their distinct contributions to the final blend. Younger brandies may offer vibrant fruit flavors and freshness, while older brandies provide depth, richness, and complexity. Blenders carefully select and combine these expressions, creating a symphony of flavors and aromas that evolve and unfold on the palate.

Blending is not just about combining different distillates and ages; it also involves the consideration of the desired flavor profile. Blenders strive to achieve a balance of fruitiness, oak influence, sweetness, and other desired characteristics. They experiment with different proportions, adjusting and fine-tuning the blend until they achieve a composition that meets their artistic vision. The artistry of blending extends beyond the technical aspects of flavor combinations. It encompasses the vision, creativity, and passion of the blender, which seeks to create a brandy that tells a story, evokes emotions, and captivates the senses. It is through their skill and artistry that brandy enthusiasts are treated to an extraordinary sensory experience.

Master blenders are the guiding hand behind the creation of exceptional brandies. They are the custodians of tradition, craftsmanship, and innovation, responsible for ensuring the continuity of quality and style in their brand's offerings.

The role of a master blender goes beyond technical expertise; it requires a deep connection to the brand's heritage, a passion for the craft, and an unwavering commitment to excellence. These skilled artisans possess an intimate knowledge of the brand's distillates, their individual characteristics, and their potential for blending.

Master blenders carefully select distillates that showcase the brand's identity while maintaining consistency. They assess and evaluate each distillate, determining its suitability for the desired blend. With their expert noses and palates, they identify the subtle nuances and complexities that make each distillate unique.

A crucial aspect of a master blender's role is the ability to balance different age expressions. They have a keen understanding of how different age statements contribute to the overall character and complexity of the brandy. Through meticulous trial and error, they create blends that capture the essence of the brand while showcasing the depth and refinement that come with age. The mastery of a master blender lies in its ability to maintain a consistent flavor profile over time. This is particularly important for brands that have established loyal followings and have built a reputation for their distinct style. Master blenders meticulously ensure that each batch of brandy adheres to the brand's signature flavor profile, even as the availability of certain distillates or age expressions may vary.

The expertise of a master blender is honed over years of experience and a deep understanding of the brandy-making process. They possess a remarkable sensory memory that allows them to detect even the slightest variations in aroma, taste, and texture. This keen sense of perception enables them to make informed decisions during the blending process, ensuring that each blend meets the brand's standards of excellence.

Master blenders also play a vital role in innovation and the exploration of new flavor profiles. They push boundaries, experimenting with different distillates, cask finishes, and aging techniques to create unique expressions that captivate the palate. Their creative vision, coupled with their technical knowledge, allows them to push the art of blending forward while staying true to the brand's identity. The influence of a master blender extends beyond the confines of the distillery. They are ambassadors for the brand, sharing their expertise and passion with consumers, industry professionals, and enthusiasts alike. Their dedication to the craft and their ability to consistently produce exceptional blends contribute to the brand's reputation and legacy.

Brandy enthusiasts are not only drawn to the brand itself but also to the master blender behind it. They appreciate the skill, artistry, and dedication that goes into every bottle. The master blender's ability to strike the perfect balance between tradition and innovation while consistently delivering outstanding blends is what sets them apart as true artisans in the world of brandy.

In conclusion, master blenders are the maestros of the brandy world, orchestrating a symphony of flavors, aromas, and textures through their expertise and artistry. Their ability to balance different distillates, ages, and flavor profiles is a testament to their profound understanding of the craft. With each blend they create, master blenders leave an indelible mark on the brand's legacy, elevating brandy to new heights of excellence and captivating the senses of enthusiasts around the world.

Styles and Varieties

Brandy is a diverse and captivating spirit, with different styles and varieties originating from various regions around the world. Each style has its unique characteristics, production methods, and flavor profiles, offering brandy enthusiasts a rich tapestry of options to explore.

Cognac: Cognac is arguably the most renowned and prestigious style of brandy. It hails from the Cognac region in southwestern France and is produced using specific grape varieties, primarily Ugni Blanc. Cognac undergoes double distillation and is aged in French oak barrels. It is known for its elegance, finesse, and complex flavor profile, often featuring notes of dried fruits, vanilla, oak, and delicate floral nuances.

Armagnac: Another esteemed French brandy, Armagnac, originates from the Gascony region in southwestern France. Unlike Cognac, Armagnac is typically distilled only once, resulting in a more robust and rustic character. It is often crafted using grape varieties such as Ugni Blanc, Folle Blanche, and Colombard. Armagnac exhibits a wide range of flavors, including dried fruits, spices, chocolate, and earthy undertones.

Fruit Brandies: Fruit brandies encompass a broad category of brandies made from various fruits other than grapes. These brandies showcase the distinct characteristics of the fruit used in their production. For example, apple brandy (Calvados) from Normandy, France, captures the essence of apples with a balance of sweetness and acidity. Pear brandy (Poire William) from Switzerland and Germany highlights the delicate aroma and flavor of pears.

Cherry brandy (Kirsch) from Germany and Slovenia offers the intense, rich flavors of cherries.

Other Regional Brandies: Brandies are produced in many other regions worldwide, each with its own unique style and characteristics. Spanish brandy, such as Brandy de Jerez, is known for its rich and full-bodied nature, often aged in sherry casks. Greek brandy, known as Metaxa, combines aged brandy with Muscat wine to create a distinct aromatic profile. American brandies, including those from California and Kentucky, showcase the country's innovative approach to brandy production, often incorporating unique grape varieties and aging techniques.

Cognac is produced through a meticulous process that begins with the harvest and fermentation of specific grape varieties. The wine resulting from this fermentation is then distilled twice using traditional copper pot stills. The distillate is aged in French oak barrels, typically for a minimum of two years, with longer aging periods producing more complex and refined expressions. Cognac exhibits a harmonious blend of fruity, floral, and oaky notes with a smooth and velvety texture.

Armagnac follows a similar production process to Cognac but is distilled only once using column stills or traditional Alembic stills. This single distillation method preserves more of the grape's natural flavors and aromas, resulting in a more robust and intense brandy. Armagnac is aged in French oak barrels, often for extended periods, allowing it to develop rich and complex flavors of dried fruits, spices, and earthy undertones.

Fruit brandies are typically produced by fermenting the fruit's juice or pulp, followed by distillation. The choice of fruit, fermentation techniques, and distillation methods vary depending on the region and traditions associated with each fruit brandy. For example, apple brandy (Calvados) is made by fermenting apple cider and then subjecting it to double distillation. It is aged in oak barrels, allowing the flavors to mellow and develop complexity over time. The resulting brandy exhibits a balanced combination of fruity sweetness, subtle acidity, and a hint of apple orchard aromas.

Pear brandy (Poire William) is crafted by fermenting the juice of pears and then distilling it in copper stills. It is often aged in stainless steel or glass containers to preserve its delicate flavor and aroma. Pear brandy is known for its smoothness, floral notes, and the essence of ripe pears.

Cherry brandy (Kirsch) is made by fermenting and distilling cherries, capturing their vibrant flavors. It is commonly consumed as a clear, colorless brandy with intense cherry aromas and a rich, fruity taste. Cherries used for Kirsch are often carefully selected and crushed with their pits to extract maximum flavor.

Other Regional Brandies: Spanish brandy, such as Brandy de Jerez, follows the Solera aging system, which involves blending brandies of different ages to achieve consistency and complexity. The brandy is aged in oak casks previously used for sherry, imparting unique characteristics. Brandy de Jerez exhibits flavors of dried fruit, spices, and hints of oak, with a velvety texture.

Greek brandy, specifically Metaxa, is produced by blending aged grape brandy with Muscat wine and a secret blend of botanicals. This results in a distinctive aromatic profile with notes of citrus, herbs, and floral elements. Metaxa is aged in oak barrels to enhance its flavor complexity and smoothness. American brands offer a range of styles and production methods. California brandies often utilize a variety of grape varieties and employ modern distillation techniques, resulting in expressive and fruit-forward expressions. Kentucky brandies, influenced by the bourbon tradition, may be aged in charred oak barrels, showcasing robust flavors, hints of vanilla, and a touch of oak.

Each style of brandy has its own allure and charm, reflecting the traditions, terroir, and craftsmanship of the region in which it is produced. Exploring these different styles allows brandy enthusiasts to experience the breadth of flavors and aromas that the world of brandy has to offer. The world of brandy encompasses a captivating array of styles and varieties, each with its unique characteristics and production methods. From the refined elegance of Cognac and Armagnac to the fruit-forward expressions of apple, pear, and cherry brandies, there is a brandy to suit every palate. Understanding the distinct qualities and flavor profiles associated with each style enhances the appreciation and enjoyment of this timeless spirit. Whether sipped neat, enjoyed in cocktails, or paired with culinary delights, brandy offers a sensory journey that celebrates the rich heritage and artistry of the distiller's craft.

Tasting and Appreciation

Tasting brandy is an art form that engages the senses and allows us to fully appreciate the complex flavors and aromas that this noble spirit has to offer. So, grab your favorite brandy glass, sit back, and let's embark on a delightful journey of sensory exploration.

Glassware: First things first, the choice of glassware can greatly enhance your brandy-tasting experience. Opt for a tulip-shaped glass with a narrow opening. This design helps concentrate the aromas, allowing you to fully appreciate the bouquet. Plus, it makes you feel fancy, and let's face it, sipping brandy is all about feeling a bit fancy, isn't it?

Appearance: Take a moment to observe the brandy's appearance. Hold the glass up to the light and admire its beautiful color and clarity. Swirl it gently and watch as the liquid coats the glass, forming "legs" or "tears." These are not just fancy aesthetics; they provide clues about the brandy's viscosity and age. The thicker and slower the tears, the higher the alcohol content and the more aged the brandy.

Now, let's move on to the most exciting part—the tasting itself!

Note: Before taking that first sip, bring the glass close to your nose and take a deep breath. Inhale the exquisite aromas and let them tickle your olfactory senses. You might detect a symphony of scents, from ripe fruits to delicate floral notes, from spices to hints of oak. It's like a fragrant fireworks display in your nostrils.

Palate: Take a small sip and let the brandy coat your palate. Swirl it around, allowing it to touch every taste bud. Notice the flavors that unfold—the luscious sweetness of fruits, the warmth of spices, the gentle caress of vanilla, and perhaps a whisper of caramel or chocolate. Let the flavors dance on your tongue like a well-choreographed tango.

Finish: As you swallow, pay attention to the brandy's finish. Does it linger gracefully, leaving a pleasant warmth and a delightful aftertaste? A long and satisfying finish is a sign of a well-crafted brandy, one that deserves an appreciative nod and maybe even a little applause.

Remember, the key to fully enjoying brandy is to savor each sip, allowing yourself to be transported by its flavors and aromas. Take your time, explore different brands and styles, and discover the ones that truly resonate with your taste preferences. Whether you're a brandy connoisseur or a curious beginner, there's a world of pleasure waiting to be discovered in every bottle. So, raise your glass, toast to the magic of brandy, and embrace the joy of tasting this exquisite spirit. Cheers to good times, good friends, and unforgettable brandy experiences!

CHAPTER 6-TROUBLESHOOTING AND COMMON MISTAKES

When it comes to home distilling, even experienced distillers can run into issues from time to time. Understanding common mistakes and knowing how to troubleshoot problems can greatly improve your success rate. In this section, we will discuss some common issues that arise during the distillation process and provide solutions to help you overcome them.

- **Poor Fermentation**

One of the most common mistakes in home distilling is a poor fermentation process. If the fermentation is not carried out properly, it can lead to off-flavors and low alcohol yields. Here are a few common issues and how to address them:

Insufficient yeast pitch: If you don't add enough yeast to the fermentation, it can result in a sluggish fermentation or no fermentation at all. Ensure you follow the recommended yeast pitching rates and use a quality yeast strain suitable for the type of spirit you're making.

Inadequate nutrient levels: Yeast requires essential nutrients to thrive and produce alcohol. If your fermentation is sluggish, it could be due to a lack of nutrients. Consider using yeast nutrients or adding nutrient-rich ingredients like fruit or grain to the fermentation.

Improper temperature control: Yeast is sensitive to temperature fluctuations. If the fermentation temperature is too low, the yeast activity will slow down, while high temperatures can stress the yeast or even kill it. Maintain the recommended temperature range for your chosen yeast strain.

- **Off-Flavors and Spoilage**

Obtaining a high-quality spirit requires careful attention to detail throughout the distillation process. However, sometimes off-flavors or spoilage can occur. Here's how to prevent and address these issues:

Contamination: Contamination can happen at various stages, such as during fermentation or distillation. Make sure to sanitize all equipment properly and maintain a clean distilling environment. Regularly clean and sterilize your equipment to minimize the risk of contamination.

Fusel alcohols: Fusel alcohols are undesirable compounds that can cause harsh flavors and aromas in your distilled spirits. They are often produced when the fermentation temperature is too high or when the yeast is stressed. Control the fermentation temperature within the recommended range to minimize the formation of fuel alcohols.

Heads and tails separation: During distillation, it's essential to separate the heads (containing undesirable compounds) and tails (lower alcohol content) from the heart of the distillate. Failing to do so can result in off-flavors. Learn to recognize the different stages of distillation and make appropriate cuts to ensure a clean and flavorful spirit.

Aging: If your spirit still has off-flavors after distillation, consider aging it in oak barrels. The wood can help mellow harsh flavors and enhance the overall character of the spirit.

- **Sanitation and Cleanliness:**

Maintaining a clean and sanitized environment is crucial for preventing off-flavors and spoilage. Always clean and sanitize your equipment thoroughly before and after each use, including fermenters, stills, hoses, and storage containers. Use food-grade sanitizers recommended for home distilling and rinse all equipment with hot water to ensure no residual sanitizing agents remain.

- **Ingredient Quality and Storage**

The quality of your ingredients greatly impacts the flavor and overall quality of your spirits. Ensure you are using high-quality grains, fruits, or other raw materials, as any defects or spoilage can negatively affect the final product. Store your ingredients properly in a cool, dry place to prevent mold growth or degradation.

- **Yeast Health and Fermentation Control**

Maintaining a healthy fermentation process is crucial for preventing off-flavors and spoilage. Choose a yeast strain suitable for the spirit you're producing and ensure proper yeast hydration and rehydration. Monitor the fermentation temperature closely, as excessively high temperatures can produce unwanted flavors. Proper yeast nutrient additions and pH control will promote healthy yeast growth and minimize the risk of off-flavors.

Troubleshooting Distillation Problems

Distillation can sometimes present challenges, but with proper troubleshooting, you can overcome them. Here are a few common distillation problems and their solutions:

Low alcohol yield: If you're obtaining a low alcohol yield, it could be due to various factors such as insufficient fermentation, improper temperature control, or incorrect setup of your distillation apparatus. Review your fermentation process and equipment setup to identify any potential issues.

Poor separation of alcohol: If you're not getting a clean separation of alcohol during distillation, it might be due to incorrect temperature control, faulty equipment, or improper collection of the distillate. Ensure that your still is properly calibrated, and adjust the temperature carefully to achieve optimal separation.

Cloudy distillate: Cloudy distillate can be caused by various factors, including excess solids or impurities carried over during distillation. Consider using filtration techniques or allowing the distillate to settle and clarify before bottling. Filtration methods such as activated carbon or charcoal filters can help remove impurities and improve the clarity of your spirit.

Smearing: Smearing refers to the presence of off-flavors or impurities throughout the distillate rather than being limited to heads or tails. It can be caused by factors such as improper temperature control, poor fermentation, or a faulty still design. Carefully review your distillation process, including fermentation, temperature control, and the configuration of your still, to identify and address the source of the smearing issue.

Proper Storage and Aging Techniques

Proper storage and aging are crucial steps in the production of premium vodka, whiskey, and brandy. Here are some guidelines to ensure optimal results:

Choosing the Right Containers: Select appropriate containers for aging based on the spirit you're producing. For whiskey and brandy, oak barrels are the traditional choice, as they impart desirable flavors and facilitate the aging process. Make sure the barrels are charred or toasted to allow for better interaction between the spirit and wood. For vodka, stainless steel or glass containers are commonly used.

Controlling Storage Conditions: Maintain consistent and appropriate storage conditions to promote aging and flavor development. For whiskey and brandy, aim for a temperature range of 12-20°C (54-68°F) and a humidity level of around 60-70%. Vodka, being a neutral spirit, is less influenced by aging and can be stored at room temperature.

Aging Duration: The duration of aging depends on personal preference and the desired flavor profile. Whiskey and brandy typically benefit from longer aging periods to develop complex flavors and smoothness. However, remember that over-aging can lead to excessive wood influence, so it's essential to taste periodic and monitor the development.

Tasting and Sampling

Regularly sample your aged spirits to monitor their progress and ensure they are developing as desired. This allows you to make adjustments or decide when the spirits have reached the desired flavor profile. Use a standardized testing process to evaluate aroma, flavor, and overall balance. By following these storage and aging techniques, you can enhance the quality and character of your spirits:

- **Avoiding Light and Oxygen Exposure**: Light and oxygen can have detrimental effects on the flavor and stability of aged spirits. Store your barrels or containers in a dark, cool environment to minimize light exposure. Ensure a tight seal to prevent oxygen from entering the aging vessel. If using barrels, periodically check for any leaks and address them promptly.
- **Blending and Dilution:** Once your spirits have reached the desired aging period, you may choose to blend different batches or adjust the alcohol content by dilution. Blending can help achieve consistency and balance in flavor. Dilution with distilled water can bring the alcohol content to the desired level and allow the flavors to harmonize.
- **Patience and Documentation:** Aging spirits require patience as flavors develop gradually over time. Maintain detailed records of each batch, noting the date of distillation,

type of spirit, aging duration, and any other relevant observations. This documentation allows you to track the progression and make informed decisions about future batches.

- **Experimentation and Learning:** Every distilling journey is unique, and experimentation is key to refining your craft. Try different aging techniques, such as using different types of wood and char levels or incorporating additional flavors through infusions. Embrace the learning process, as it will deepen your understanding of aging characteristics and help you discover your own signature style.

By addressing common issues, preventing off-flavors and spoilage, and employing proper storage and aging techniques, you can enhance the quality and enjoyment of your home-distilled vodka, whiskey, and brandy. Remember to always prioritize safety, adhere to legal requirements, and continue learning and experimenting to refine your skills as a home distiller.

CHAPTER 7- SAFETY, LEGALITIES, AND RESPONSIBLE DISTILLING

Ensuring Safety during the Distillation Process

Distilling your own spirits can be an exciting and rewarding experience, but it is essential to prioritize safety throughout the entire process. Distillation involves working with flammable substances and operating equipment that requires careful attention and precautionary measures. In this section, we will discuss various steps and guidelines to ensure a safe distillation process.

- **Proper Equipment and Setup:**

When setting up your home distillation apparatus, it is crucial to use equipment specifically designed for distilling purposes. Ensure that you still are made of food-grade materials such as copper or stainless steel, as other metals may contaminate the final product. Follow the manufacturer's instructions for assembling and operating the still, as each model may have specific requirements.

- **Ventilation:**

Distillation produces alcohol vapor, which can be hazardous if inhaled in large quantities. It is vital to perform distillation in a well-ventilated area, preferably outdoors or in a dedicated distilling room with proper ventilation systems. Adequate airflow will help dissipate any potentially harmful vapors and reduce the risk of fire or explosion.

- **Fire Safety:**

Due to the flammable nature of alcohol and the presence of open flames during distillation, fire safety precautions are of utmost importance. Keep a fire extinguisher nearby and ensure it is in good working condition. Do not leave the still unattended while it is in operation, and keep a watchful eye on the heating source, whether it's an open flame or an electric element.

- **Temperature Control:**

Maintaining precise temperature control throughout the distillation process is crucial for the safety and quality of your spirits. Follow the temperature guidelines provided by the recipe or instructions for the specific type of spirit you are distilling. Overheating can lead to the production of harmful compounds, or even cause the distillate to ignite, so it is essential to monitor and adjust the temperature as needed.

- **Water Supply and Cooling:**

During distillation, the vapor produced needs to be condensed back into a liquid form. This requires a reliable water supply for cooling purposes. Ensure that you have a sufficient water source and that your condenser is properly connected and functioning correctly. Regularly check for leaks or blockages that could compromise the cooling process.

- **Handling Flammable Materials:**

Throughout the distillation process, you will be working with high-proof alcohol, which is highly flammable. Take extra precautions when handling and storing these materials. Keep them away from open flames, sparks, or any potential ignition sources. Store them in a cool, dry place, preferably in tightly sealed containers specifically designed for storing high-proof spirits.

- **Personal Protective Equipment (PPE):**

Wearing appropriate personal protective equipment (PPE) is essential for ensuring your safety during distillation. When operating the still, consider wearing heat-resistant gloves, safety glasses, and protective clothing to minimize the risk of burns or exposure to harmful substances. PPE will provide an additional layer of protection in case of accidents or mishaps.

- **Emergency Preparedness:**

Despite taking all necessary precautions, accidents can still happen. It is crucial to be prepared for potential emergencies. Familiarize yourself with the location of emergency exits and have a first aid kit readily available. Make sure you know how to use the fire extinguisher effectively and have a plan in place to contact emergency services if needed.

- **Education and Training:**

Before embarking on the journey of home distilling, it is essential to educate yourself about the process thoroughly. Gain a comprehensive understanding of the science behind distillation, including the principles of vaporization, condensation, and purification. Research reputable sources, attend workshops or classes, and connect with experienced distillers who can provide valuable insights and guidance. The more knowledgeable you are, the better equipped you will be to ensure safety during the distillation process.

- **Distillation Batch Size:**

It is crucial to consider the batch size when distilling at home. Working with smaller batches is generally recommended for several reasons, including safety. By distilling in smaller quantities, you have better control over the process and can more easily manage temperature fluctuations, prevent potential accidents, and maintain a safer working environment. Additionally, smaller batches allow for more precise flavor adjustments and experimentation.

- **Risk of Methanol:**

Methanol is a toxic substance that can be produced during the distillation process, especially when using certain raw materials. It is crucial to be aware of the risks associated with methanol and take appropriate measures to minimize its formation. Avoid using questionable or unknown sources of ingredients, as they may contain higher levels of methanol. Always discard the "heads" and "tails" of the distillate, as these portions often contain higher concentrations of methanol. Proper separation of the methanol-rich portions from the desired ethanol is essential to ensure the safety of your homemade spirits.

- **Cleanliness and Sanitation:**

Maintaining a clean and sanitary distilling environment is crucial for both the safety and the quality of your spirits. Before starting the distillation process, thoroughly clean and sanitize all equipment, including the still, fermenters, and any other utensils you will be using. Proper sanitation reduces the risk of contamination and ensures that your spirits are free from unwanted bacteria or impurities.

- **Avoiding Contamination:**

To prevent contamination, it is important to handle ingredients and equipment with clean hands or gloves. Avoid introducing foreign substances into the distilling process, such as dirt, dust, or unclean water. Store your ingredients properly, ensuring they are sealed and protected from potential contaminants. Regularly inspect and clean your equipment to maintain its integrity and prevent any buildup of residues that could affect the quality of your spirits.

- **Regular Maintenance and Inspections:**

Performing regular maintenance and inspections of your distillation equipment is crucial for safety. Check for any signs of wear and tear, such as loose connections, leaks, or faulty components. Regularly clean and replace any parts that show signs of deterioration. By conducting routine inspections, you can identify and address any potential safety hazards before they escalate.

- **Responsible Monitoring:**

During the distillation process, it is important to monitor the operation continuously. Stay vigilant and observe any unusual smells, sounds, or visual cues that may indicate a problem. If you notice anything out of the ordinary, such as excessive pressure, leaks, or unexpected fluctuations in temperature, take immediate action to address the issue or stop the process if necessary. Regular monitoring ensures that you can quickly respond to any safety concerns that may arise.

Remember, safety should always be the top priority when engaging in home distilling. By following these guidelines and incorporating responsible practices into your distillation process, you can enjoy the art of crafting your own spirits while ensuring a safe and enjoyable experience.

Legal regulations and permits for home distilling

Distilling alcohol at home is subject to various legal regulations and permits that vary from country to country and even within different regions. It is crucial to understand and comply with the applicable laws to ensure that you are engaging in home distilling within the bounds of the law. In this section, we will explore the general legal considerations and permits associated with home distilling.

- **Research Local Laws:**

Before you begin distilling, thoroughly research the laws and regulations regarding home distilling in your specific jurisdiction. Laws can differ significantly, and it is essential to familiarize yourself with the legal requirements in your area. Look for information provided by government agencies responsible for alcohol control or taxation, as well as local licensing bodies.

- **Legalization of Home Distilling:**

Some countries permit home distilling for personal use, while others strictly prohibit it altogether. In certain jurisdictions, there may be quantity limits on the amount of alcohol you can produce for personal consumption. Determine whether home distilling is legal in your country and whether there are any specific restrictions or conditions associated with it.

- **Licensing and Permits:**

In regions where home distilling is legal, you may be required to obtain specific licenses or permits to engage in the activity. These licenses are typically aimed at regulating the production, distribution, and taxation of alcohol. Check with your local alcohol control board or regulatory agency to determine if any permits are necessary and what the application process entails.

- **Personal Consumption vs. Distribution:**

Most legal frameworks for home distilling focus on allowing individuals to produce alcohol for personal use rather than for commercial purposes. The distinction between personal consumption and distribution can vary, so be aware of the limits on sharing or selling your homemade spirits. Engaging in the sale or distribution of homemade spirits without the necessary permits may be illegal and subject to penalties.

- **Age Restrictions:**

Legal regulations often include age restrictions on engaging in home distilling. In many countries, the minimum legal drinking age also applies to the production of alcohol. Ensure that you are of legal drinking age in your jurisdiction before embarking on the home distilling process.

- **Labeling and Bottling Requirements:**

Even if home distilling is legal in your area, there may be specific labeling and bottling requirements that you need to comply with. These requirements typically include information such as alcohol content, ingredients, warnings, and contact details. Research the regulations pertaining to labeling and packaging and ensure that your homemade spirits meet the necessary standards.

- **Reporting and Tax Obligations:**

In some regions, there may be tax obligations associated with home distilling. This can include reporting the quantity of alcohol produced, paying excise taxes, or obtaining a license as a small-scale producer. Familiarize yourself with the tax regulations in your jurisdiction and comply with any reporting or payment obligations to avoid legal issues.

- **Compliance with Safety Standards:**

Alongside legal regulations, it is important to adhere to safety standards when it comes to home distilling. While safety practices were covered in the previous section, ensuring that your distillation process meets safety standards may also be a requirement for obtaining permits or licenses. This can involve demonstrating proper equipment setup, ventilation systems, and adherence to fire safety protocols.

- **Staying Updated:**

Laws and regulations surrounding home distilling may change over time. It is crucial to stay updated on any legislative updates or revisions that may impact your home distilling activities. Regularly check for updates from local authorities or join relevant forums or associations to stay informed about changes in regulations.

- **Seek Legal Advice:**

If you are unsure about the specific legal requirements or permits for home distilling in your area, it is advisable to consult with a legal professional who specializes in alcohol regulations. They can provide guidance based on your specific circumstances and help you navigate the legal landscape effectively.

- **Compliance with Health and Safety Standards:**

In addition to legal regulations, there may be health and safety standards that you need to comply with when distilling alcohol at home. These standards may include guidelines for handling ingredients, sanitation practices, and product quality control. Familiarize yourself with any applicable health and safety regulations to ensure that your homemade spirits meet the necessary standards.

- **Community Restrictions and Noise Considerations:**

Depending on where you live, there may be community restrictions or noise considerations that could impact your ability to engage in home distilling. Check if there are any local ordinances, or homeowner association rules that restrict or regulate the production of alcohol on residential properties. Being mindful of your neighbors' concerns and respecting noise regulations can help maintain positive relationships within your community.

- **Liability and Insurance:**

When engaging in home distilling, it is essential to consider liability and insurance coverage. While not mandatory in all jurisdictions, obtaining liability insurance can provide protection in case of accidents or injuries related to your home distilling activities. Consult with an insurance professional to understand the options available and determine the coverage that best suits your needs.

- **International Regulations:**

If you plan to travel or move to a different country with your homemade spirits, be aware that international regulations may differ significantly. Some countries may prohibit the importation of homemade alcohol, while others may have specific requirements or restrictions. Research and comply with the customs and alcohol import regulations of the destination country to avoid any legal complications.

- **Ethical Considerations:**

Beyond legal obligations, ethical considerations are important when it comes to home distilling. Respecting intellectual property rights and avoiding the infringement of trademarks or copyrighted materials is crucial. Furthermore, practicing responsible production, consumption, and sharing of your homemade spirits promotes ethical behavior within the home distilling community.

By understanding and adhering to the legal regulations and permits associated with home distilling, you can ensure that you operate within the boundaries of the law while enjoying the art of crafting your own spirits. Remember that legal compliance, responsible practices, and respect for safety standards and regulations are key elements of being a responsible home distiller.

Responsible Consumption and Sharing of Homemade Spirits

While the process of distilling your own spirits can be exciting and rewarding, it is important to approach the consumption and sharing of homemade spirits with responsibility and care. In this section, we will explore guidelines for responsible consumption and the responsible sharing of your homemade spirits.

- **Know Your Limits:**

Alcohol affects individuals differently, and it is essential to be aware of your own tolerance and limits. Understand how alcohol impacts your body and be mindful of the recommended guidelines for safe and moderate consumption. Know when to stop and avoid excessive or binge drinking, as it can lead to adverse health effects and impaired judgment.

- **Educate Yourself and Others:**

Take the time to educate yourself and others about responsible drinking habits and the potential risks associated with alcohol consumption. Share information about standard drink sizes, alcohol content, and the effects of alcohol on the body. Encourage open conversations about responsible drinking within your social circle, promoting a culture of moderation and awareness.

- **Avoid Underage Consumption:**

Homemade spirits should never be shared with or consumed by individuals who are underage. It is crucial to adhere to the legal drinking age in your jurisdiction and to prevent access to alcohol by minors. Make sure your homemade spirits are stored securely and out of reach of underage individuals to ensure their safety.

- **Quality Control:**

As a home distiller, it is your responsibility to ensure the quality and safety of the spirits you produce. Regularly test and evaluate your homemade spirits to ensure that they meet the desired standards in terms of taste, aroma, and alcohol content. Avoid sharing spirits that may have undergone contamination or are of subpar quality.

- **Provide Information:**

When sharing your homemade spirits with others, provide information about the alcohol content and any potential allergens or ingredients used. This allows individuals to make informed decisions about consumption and helps those with dietary restrictions or allergies to avoid any adverse reactions.

- **Encourage Responsible Hosting:**

If you choose to serve your homemade spirits at gatherings or events, promote responsible hosting practices. Offer non-alcoholic beverage options alongside your homemade spirits, provide ample food, and encourage guests to pace their drinking and drink water between alcoholic beverages. Be observant and intervene if someone appears to be intoxicated or may need assistance.

- **Respect Individual Choices:**

Respect the decisions of individuals who choose not to consume alcohol or who wish to limit their consumption. Everyone has their own personal preferences and reasons for abstaining, and it is important to create an inclusive and non-judgmental environment. Offer alternative drink options to accommodate all guests' choices and preferences.

- **Designated Drivers and Transportation:**

When hosting or attending events where alcohol is served, ensure that there are designated drivers or alternative transportation options available for those who choose not to consume alcohol or are unable to do so responsibly. Encourage guests to plan for safe transportation in advance and provide information about local transportation services or ride-sharing options.

- **Lead by Example:**

As a home distiller and host, lead by example and demonstrate responsible drinking habits. Drink in moderation, avoid excessive consumption and engage in socializing and enjoyment beyond alcohol. By setting a positive example, you encourage others to follow suit and promote responsible drinking practices within your community.

Responsible consumption and sharing of homemade spirits contribute to a safer and more enjoyable experience for all involved. By promoting moderation, educating others, and practicing responsible hosting, you can ensure that the enjoyment of your homemade spirits is accompanied by a strong commitment to personal well-being and the well-being of those around you.

Ethical Considerations in distillation
Distilling your own spirits comes with a set of ethical considerations that extend beyond legal and safety

considerations. As a responsible home distiller, it is important to be mindful of these ethical considerations and conduct your distillation activities in an ethical and conscientious manner. In this section, we will explore some key ethical considerations to keep in mind when engaging in home distillation.

- **Respect Intellectual Property Rights:**

When crafting your own spirits, it is crucial to respect intellectual property rights. Avoid using branding, logos, or designs that belong to established distilleries or spirit producers. Engage in originality and creativity when developing your brand identity, labels, and marketing materials. By respecting intellectual property rights, you contribute to a fair and ethical distillation community.

- **Transparency in Sourcing Ingredients:**

Be transparent about the sourcing of your ingredients. Whenever possible, choose high-quality, sustainable, and ethically sourced ingredients for your homemade spirits. This includes considering factors such as fair trade practices, environmental impact, and supporting local producers. By being transparent and making informed choices, you can align your distillation practices with ethical principles.

- **Responsible Use of Resources:**

Distillation requires energy, water, and other resources. As an ethical distiller, be conscious of your resource consumption and aim to minimize waste. Consider implementing energy-efficient practices, such as using energy-saving equipment or recycling cooling water. Properly dispose of waste products, such as spent grains or residues, in an environmentally responsible manner. By reducing your ecological footprint, you contribute to sustainable distillation practices.

- **Consideration for Community Impact:**

Distillation activities can have an impact on the community and surrounding environment. Be mindful of the potential noise, odors, or disruptions that may arise from your home distilling operations. Respect the concerns of your neighbors and take steps to minimize any adverse effects. Openly communicate with your community about your distillation activities, addressing any questions or concerns they may have.

- **Responsible Marketing and Advertising:**

If you choose to share or sell your homemade spirits, engage in responsible marketing and advertising practices. Ensure that your promotional materials and messaging comply with relevant laws and regulations. Avoid making false or misleading claims about the quality, health benefits, or origins of your spirits. Promote your products honestly and transparently, allowing consumers to make informed choices.

- **Supporting Responsible Consumption:**

While you have control over the production of your homemade spirits, it is important to acknowledge that responsible consumption ultimately lies with the individual. Encourage responsible drinking habits, moderation, and awareness among those who consume your spirits. Promote a culture of enjoying spirits in a responsible and balanced manner, highlighting the importance of health, safety, and well-being.

- **Collaboration and Community Engagement:**

Engage with the wider distillation community and contribute positively to its growth and development. Share knowledge, experiences, and insights with fellow distillers, fostering a supportive and collaborative environment. Participate in local events or initiatives that promote responsible distillation and educate others about the craft. By actively engaging with the community, you contribute to the ethical and sustainable growth of the distillation culture.

- **Giving Credit to Inspirations and Mentors:**

As a home distiller, it is common to draw inspiration from other distillers, mentors, or educational resources. When appropriate, acknowledge and give credit to those who have influenced your distillation techniques, recipes, or overall knowledge. This not only shows respect for their expertise but also fosters a sense of gratitude and recognition within the distillation community.

- **Social Responsibility:**

Consider the broader social impact of your distillation activities. Be aware of any cultural or social sensitivities related to the consumption of alcohol in your community. Avoid promoting excessive or irresponsible drinking behaviors through your homemade spirits. Instead, encourage responsible and enjoyable experiences that promote social bonding, celebration, and appreciation of the craft.

- **Continuous Learning and Improvement:**

Ethical distillation involves a commitment to continuous learning and improvement. Stay updated on industry trends, advancements in distillation techniques, and new knowledge about ingredients or production methods. Strive to enhance your skills, refine your recipes, and develop a deeper understanding of the art and science of distillation. Embrace a growth mindset and actively seek opportunities for self-improvement.

- **Giving Back to the Community:**

Consider giving back to the community in ways that align with your distillation activities. This could involve participating in charity events, fundraisers or donating a portion of your proceeds to a cause you care about. Engage in socially responsible initiatives that contribute positively to society and use your distillation skills as a force for good.

- **Responsible Waste Management:**

Distillation generates by-products such as spent grains, residues, or distillation waste. Dispose of these materials responsibly, following local regulations and guidelines for waste management. Explore eco-friendly options, such as composting or repurposing, to minimize waste and promote sustainability. By taking responsibility for your waste management, you contribute to a cleaner and healthier environment.

- **Encouraging Sustainable Practices:**

Consider adopting sustainable practices in your distillation process. This may involve using renewable energy sources, minimizing water usage, or exploring eco-friendly packaging options. Embrace environmentally conscious choices that reduce your ecological footprint and demonstrate a commitment to sustainability in distillation.

- **Honesty and Integrity:**

Maintain a high level of honesty and integrity in your distillation journey. Be transparent about your processes, ingredients, and production methods. Avoid misleading claims or misrepresentation of your homemade spirits. Build trust with your customers, fellow distillers, and the wider community by conducting yourself with integrity and operating in an ethical manner.

By embracing these ethical considerations, you contribute to the overall integrity, sustainability, and reputation of the home distilling community. Ethical distillation practices go hand in hand with responsible and enjoyable consumption, fostering a culture of respect, transparency, and positive engagement within the distillation community and beyond.

Guidelines for Responsible Drinking

Responsible drinking is an important aspect of enjoying homemade spirits and ensuring the well-being and safety of oneself and others. By following these guidelines, you can promote a culture of responsible drinking and make the most out of your homemade spirits without compromising your health or safety.

- **Set Personal Limits:**

Understand your personal limits and drink within them. Know how much alcohol you can safely consume without experiencing negative effects. Factors such as body weight, metabolism, and tolerance levels can vary among individuals. Respect your limits and avoid exceeding them to maintain control over your drinking.

- **Pace Yourself:**

Sip and savor your homemade spirits slowly. Give your body time to process the alcohol and gauge its effects. Avoid rapid or excessive drinking, as it can lead to intoxication and impair your judgment and coordination. Take breaks between drinks and alternate with non-alcoholic beverages to stay hydrated and pace your consumption.

- **Know Standard Drink Sizes:**

Be aware of what constitutes a standard drink size. Different types of alcohol and serving sizes can vary in alcohol content. Familiarize yourself with standard measurements and alcohol by volume (ABV) percentages to make informed choices. This knowledge helps you monitor and regulate your alcohol intake accurately.

- **Avoid Drinking and Driving:**

Never drink and drive. Alcohol impairs your judgment, coordination, and reaction time, making it dangerous to operate a vehicle. Plan ahead for alternative transportation options if you anticipate consuming alcohol. Designate a sober driver, use ride-sharing services, or take public transportation to ensure your safety and the safety of others on the road.

- **Respect Others' Choices:**

Respect the choices of individuals who choose not to drink or prefer to abstain from alcohol. Avoid pressuring others to drink or making them uncomfortable with their decisions. Create an inclusive and supportive environment where everyone feels respected and included, regardless of their drinking preferences.

- **Avoid Underage Drinking:**

Homemade spirits should never be provided to or consumed by individuals who are underage. It is crucial to comply with the legal drinking age in your jurisdiction and prevent access to alcohol by minors. Ensure that your homemade spirits are stored securely and out of reach of underage individuals to promote their safety.

- **Monitor Your Intoxication Level:**

Be aware of the signs of intoxication and monitor your own alcohol consumption. Pay attention to changes in your behavior, coordination, or judgment. If you feel intoxicated, consider slowing down or stopping your drinking. It's important to maintain control over your actions and make responsible decisions.

- **Be Mindful of Medications and Health Conditions:**

If you take medications or have underlying health conditions, be mindful of how alcohol may interact with them. Some medications can have adverse effects when combined with alcohol. Consult with your healthcare provider or pharmacist to understand any potential interactions and make informed choices regarding alcohol consumption.

- **Drink with Food:**

Consuming homemade spirits with food can help slow the absorption of alcohol into your system. Enjoy your spirits as part of a meal or snack, which can also enhance the flavor pairing and overall experience. Eating while drinking helps mitigate the effects of alcohol and promotes responsible drinking.

- **Watch Out for Warning Signs:**

Be attentive to warning signs of alcohol-related issues, such as developing a tolerance, experiencing cravings, or experiencing negative consequences due to alcohol consumption. If you notice any of these signs, it may be a good idea to reassess your drinking habits and seek support if needed.

- **Take Breaks and Hydrate:**

Intermittently take breaks from drinking alcoholic beverages to give your body time to process the alcohol. Use this time to hydrate yourself by drinking water or other non-alcoholic beverages. Hydration helps counteract the dehydrating effects of alcohol and can reduce the risk of experiencing unpleasant symptoms such as a hangover.

- **Avoid Peer Pressure:**

Do not succumb to peer pressure when it comes to drinking. Make choices based on your personal preferences, limits, and well-being. It's okay to decline a drink or choose non-alcoholic alternatives if you don't feel like consuming alcohol or if you've reached your limit. Surround yourself with supportive friends who respect your choices.

- **Stay Mindful of Alcohol's Effects:**

Stay mindful of how alcohol affects your body and mind. It can impair judgment, coordination, and reaction time. It can also intensify emotions and lead to risky behaviors. Recognize these effects and make responsible decisions to ensure your safety and the safety of those around you.

- **Look Out for Others:**

Be attentive to the well-being of others when drinking. If you notice someone displaying signs of intoxication or experiencing distress, intervene and offer assistance. Encourage them to drink water, find a safe place to rest, or seek medical help if necessary. Being a responsible drinker means looking out for the well-being of your friends and acquaintances.

- **Plan Ahead:**

Plan your drinking occasions in advance to ensure responsible consumption. Consider factors such as the duration of the event, transportation arrangements, and the availability of non-alcoholic options. Setting limits and sticking to a plan can help you maintain control and avoid excessive drinking.

- **Seek Support if Needed:**

If you find it challenging to maintain responsible drinking habits or if you're concerned about your relationship with alcohol, don't hesitate to seek support. Talk to a healthcare professional, counselor, or support group specializing in alcohol-related issues. They can provide guidance, resources, and strategies to help you make positive changes.

- **Educate Others:**

Take the opportunity to educate others about responsible drinking habits. Share your knowledge and experiences with friends, family, and the community. Promote awareness about the risks of excessive alcohol consumption and the benefits of moderation. By spreading the message of responsible drinking, you can contribute to a healthier drinking culture.

- **Reflect on Your Drinking Choices:**

Periodically reflect on your own drinking habits and evaluate whether they align with your goals and values. Assess the impact of alcohol on your life, relationships, and overall well-being. Make adjustments as necessary to ensure that your drinking habits remain responsible and aligned with your personal values.

By adhering to these guidelines for responsible drinking, you can cultivate a positive and balanced relationship with your homemade spirits. Remember, responsible drinking is about enjoying the experience while prioritizing your health, safety, and the well-being of those around you.

Safe Handling and Storage of Homemade Spirits

Ensuring the safe handling and storage of your homemade spirits is essential for maintaining their quality, preserving their flavors, and preventing any potential hazards. By following these guidelines, you can safeguard your spirits and promote a safe environment for yourself and others.

- **Clean and Sanitize Equipment:**

Before starting the distillation process, thoroughly clean and sanitize all equipment that will come into contact with your homemade spirits. This includes fermentation vessels, still components, bottles, and utensils. Use a food-grade sanitizer or a mixture of water and bleach to eliminate any bacteria or contaminants that could compromise the quality of your spirits.

- **Proper Ventilation:**

When distilling, ensure that your distillation area is well-ventilated. Proper ventilation helps prevent the buildup of potentially harmful vapors or gases. Set up your distillation apparatus in a well-ventilated room or use an appropriate ventilation system, such as a fume hood or extractor fan. This promotes a safe working environment and reduces the risk of inhalation hazards.

- **Use Safety Equipment:**

Wear appropriate safety equipment when handling homemade spirits, especially during the distillation process. This may include heat-resistant gloves, safety goggles, and protective clothing to protect yourself from potential burns or spills. Handling hot liquids and working with flammable materials requires caution and the use of proper safety gear.

- **Label and Date Bottles:**

Properly label and date your homemade spirit bottles to maintain organization and ensure that you can easily identify their contents. Include the type of spirit, the date of distillation or bottling, and any additional relevant information. Clear labeling prevents confusion and promotes safe consumption by providing accurate information about the contents.

- **Store in Suitable Containers:**

Choose suitable containers for storing your homemade spirits. Use food-grade glass bottles or containers designed for storing alcohol. Avoid using containers made of materials that may interact with or leach into the spirits, affecting their quality. Ensure that the containers have tight-fitting lids or closures to prevent evaporation or leakage.

- **Store in a Cool, Dark Place:**

Store your homemade spirits in a cool, dark place away from direct sunlight or sources of heat. Exposure to heat or light can degrade the quality of the spirits and accelerate the aging process. Optimal storage conditions help maintain the flavors and characteristics of your spirits over time.

- **Prevent Access by Minors:**

Take precautions to prevent access to your homemade spirits by individuals who are underage. Store your spirits in a secure location, such as a locked cabinet or cellar, to ensure that they are not accessible to minors. Responsible storage practices contribute to the prevention of underage drinking and promote the safety of young individuals.

- **Handle Flammable Materials Safely:**

Alcohol is highly flammable, and it is important to handle flammable materials with care. Avoid open flames, sparks, or smoking in the vicinity of your homemade spirits. Keep flammable materials, such as ethanol or high-proof spirits, away from potential ignition sources. Exercise caution to prevent accidents or fires.

- **Monitor for Spoilage or Contamination:**

Regularly monitor your homemade spirits for signs of spoilage or contamination. Look out for changes in color, unusual odors, or the presence of sediment or mold. If you notice any abnormalities, discard the affected batch to prevent the risk of consuming spoiled or contaminated spirits. Regular monitoring helps maintain the safety and quality of your homemade spirits.

- **Educate Others on Safe Handling:**

Educate those who may come into contact with your homemade spirits about safe handling practices. Inform family members, friends, or guests about the potential hazards and the importance of responsible handling. By raising awareness and providing guidance, you contribute to a safe and informed environment.

- **Be Mindful of Allergens:**

Consider the presence of allergens when handling or sharing your homemade spirits. Some individuals may have allergies or sensitivities to certain ingredients commonly used in distillation, such as grains or fruits. Clearly communicate the ingredients used in your spirits to potential consumers or guests, allowing them to make informed decisions and avoid any potential allergic reactions.

- **Dispose of Waste Properly:**

Properly dispose of any waste generated during the distillation process. This includes spent grains, residues, or discarded materials. Follow local regulations and guidelines for waste disposal to prevent environmental contamination. Consider environmentally friendly options, such as composting spent grains or repurposing waste materials whenever possible.

- **Be Cautious with Experimental Batches:**

If you venture into experimenting with new recipes or techniques, exercise caution and follow established safety protocols. Keep detailed records of your experiments, including ingredients used, measurements, and any modifications made. This documentation can be helpful for future reference, troubleshooting, and ensuring consistency in your distillation process.

- **Prevent Cross-Contamination:**

Avoid cross-contamination between different batches or types of spirits. Thoroughly clean and sanitize equipment between uses to prevent flavors, aromas, or residues from one batch from transferring to another. Cross-contamination can alter the intended characteristics of your spirits and compromise their quality.

- **Be Prepared for Emergencies:**

Maintain a basic understanding of first aid and have appropriate emergency response measures in place. Keep a fully stocked first aid kit readily available in your distillation area. Familiarize yourself with the proper procedures for handling accidents, burns, or other emergencies that may occur during the distillation process.

- **Store Flammable Materials Safely:**

If you have flammable materials such as ethanol or high-proof spirits, store them in accordance with local regulations and safety guidelines. Ensure they are stored away from potential ignition sources, in well-ventilated areas, and away from areas with high temperatures. Follow proper storage practices to minimize the risk of accidents or fires.

- **Regular Maintenance of Equipment:**

Maintain your distillation equipment by conducting regular inspections and maintenance. Check for any signs of wear and tear, leaks, or malfunctions that could pose safety hazards. Clean and sanitize your equipment regularly to prevent the buildup of contaminants and maintain the integrity of your distillation process.

- **Stay Informed on Safety Regulations:**

Stay updated on the legal and safety regulations regarding home distillation in your jurisdiction. Regulations may vary depending on your location, and it's essential to comply with the applicable laws. Stay informed about any changes or updates to ensure that your distillation activities are conducted within the legal framework and adhere to safety standards.

By adhering to these guidelines for the safe handling and storage of your homemade spirits, you can protect yourself, your creations, and those around you.

Responsibility and safety should always be at the forefront of your distillation practices, ensuring a positive and enjoyable experience for all enthusiasts of homemade spirits.

Educating Others about the Risks and Benefits

One of the responsibilities that come with being a home distiller is educating others about the risks and benefits associated with homemade spirits. By sharing your knowledge and experiences, you can contribute to a culture of informed and responsible drinking. Here are some ways to effectively educate others about the world of distillation:

- **Host Tastings and Workshops:**

Organize tastings and workshops to introduce people to the art of distillation. Provide them with a firsthand experience of the flavors, aromas, and craftsmanship involved. Share the history and process behind different spirits, highlighting the nuances that make each one unique. By engaging their senses and curiosity, you can spark an interest in homemade spirits and open up conversations about responsible drinking.

- **Emphasize Quality and Craftsmanship:**

Educate others about the meticulous attention to detail and craftsmanship that goes into producing homemade spirits. Discuss the importance of using high-quality ingredients, proper techniques, and the patience required for aging and flavor development. By highlighting the passion and dedication that home distillers put into their craft, you can foster an appreciation for the artistry and encourage responsible consumption.

- **Address Safety and Legal Considerations:**

Educate others about the safety measures and legal considerations involved in home distillation. Discuss topics such as proper equipment usage, fire safety, and adherence to local regulations. Emphasize the importance of understanding the potential risks and taking necessary precautions to ensure a safe distillation process. By promoting responsible practices, you can help prevent accidents and ensure compliance with the law.

- **Share Knowledge about Alcohol Content and Units:**

Educate individuals about alcohol content and the concept of standard drink units. Explain how the strength of homemade spirits can vary and the importance of knowing the alcohol by volume (ABV) percentage. Provide practical examples to help people understand the standard unit measurements and how to gauge their consumption accordingly. Empower them with the knowledge to make informed decisions about their alcohol intake.

- **Discuss Responsible Consumption Guidelines:**

Engage in conversations about responsible drinking guidelines, emphasizing the importance of moderation and pacing. Educate others about the potential health risks of excessive alcohol consumption and the importance of knowing their personal limits. Encourage them to enjoy homemade spirits as part of a balanced and mindful approach to drinking, appreciating the flavors without overindulging.

- **Share Tips for Flavor Pairing and Mixology:**

Educate others about the art of flavor pairing and mixology to enhance their enjoyment of homemade spirits. Discuss different cocktail recipes and suggest suitable ingredients that complement the flavors of specific spirits. Encourage responsible experimentation and discourage excessive alcohol consumption by focusing on the quality and experience of the drink.

- **Encourage Open Dialogue:**

Create a safe and non-judgmental space for open dialogue about alcohol consumption. Encourage individuals to share their thoughts, experiences, and questions about homemade spirits. Foster conversations about responsible drinking habits, challenging misconceptions, and addressing concerns. By promoting open dialogue, you can help dispel myths and provide accurate information.

- **Collaborate with Local Communities and Organizations:**

Collaborate with local community groups, alcohol awareness organizations, or responsible drinking campaigns. Offer your expertise and insights as a home distiller to support their educational initiatives. By joining forces, you can reach a broader audience and contribute to a collective effort to promote responsible drinking practices.

- **Utilize Digital Platforms:**

Leverage the power of digital platforms to educate a wider audience. Create informative and engaging content through blog posts, social media, podcasts, or YouTube videos. Share your knowledge, experiences, and tips on responsible drinking, distillation techniques, and flavor profiles. Engage with your audience, answer their questions, and foster a supportive online community centered around responsible home distilling.

- **Encourage Personal Reflection:**

Encourage individuals to reflect on their own relationship with alcohol and make informed choices based on their values and priorities. Help them understand that responsible drinking is a personal decision that should align with their individual goals and well-being. Encourage self-awareness and self-control when it comes to consuming homemade spirits.

- **Address Myths and Misconceptions:**

Take the opportunity to address common myths and misconceptions surrounding homemade spirits and responsible drinking. Dispel misconceptions that homemade spirits are inherently dangerous or that they promote excessive consumption. Provide accurate information backed by scientific knowledge and experience to help individuals make informed decisions.

- **Highlight the Social Aspect:**

Emphasize the social aspect of enjoying homemade spirits responsibly. Encourage individuals to savor the experience with friends and loved ones, engaging in meaningful conversations and connections. By focusing on the social and cultural aspects of responsible drinking, you can create a positive and enjoyable atmosphere that promotes responsible consumption.

- **Advocate for Health and Well-being:**

Educate others about the potential health benefits and risks associated with alcohol consumption. Discuss the importance of maintaining a healthy lifestyle, including regular exercise, balanced nutrition, and adequate rest. Emphasize that responsible drinking is just one aspect of overall well-being and should be approached with mindfulness and moderation.

- **Stay Updated with Research and Trends:**

As a home distiller and educator, stay updated with the latest research, trends, and best practices in the field of distillation and responsible drinking. Continuously expand your knowledge and share valuable insights with others. By staying informed, you can provide accurate and up-to-date information that contributes to a well-rounded understanding of the subject.

Remember, educating others about the risks and benefits of homemade spirits and responsible drinking is an ongoing process. Be patient, approachable, and empathetic in your discussions. Your aim is to foster a culture of knowledge, understanding, and responsible enjoyment of homemade spirits. By sharing your expertise and passion, you can inspire others to explore and appreciate the world of distillation while promoting safety and responsible consumption.

CONCLUSION

"HOME DISTILLING FOR BEGINNERS: A step by step guide to making your own fine spirits at home with easy to follow process, essential tips and mouthwatering recipes," I am filled with a profound sense of awe and reverence for the timeless art of distillation. Throughout these chapters, we have delved into the depths of this ancient craft, unraveling its secrets and unlocking the door to a world of flavors and aromas that tantalize the senses. We have shared in the joy of creation, the thrill of experimentation, and the satisfaction of witnessing the transformation of raw ingredients into liquid poetry. But beyond the recipes and techniques lies a deeper essence that binds us all—a shared connection to our roots, the art of craftsmanship, and the timeless rituals passed down through generations. In the quiet corners of our homes, we have become alchemists, weaving together science and tradition to create something unique that carries a piece of our own story.

Home distilling is not merely a means to an end but a pathway to self-discovery, creativity, and celebrating life's simple pleasures. It is an invitation to slow down, savor the process, and appreciate the quiet moments spent tending to our stills, we find solace and sanctuary—a sanctuary where time slows down, and the worries of the world fade into the background. It is within these sacred moments that we discover a profound connection to the artistry of our ancestors as we honor their legacy and carry it forward into the future.

But the true magic of home distilling lies in the spirits that grace our glasses and the bonds we forge along the way. From sharing the fruits of our labor with friends and loved ones to exchanging stories and tips with fellow enthusiasts, we have become part of a vibrant community that spans continents and cultures. We connect with kindred spirits who understand the beauty of crafting something with our own hands and the joy of sharing it with others.

And as we close this chapter, let us remember that the journey of home distilling is never-ending. There will always be new ingredients to explore, techniques to refine, and flavors to discover. It is a lifelong pursuit that rewards patience, curiosity, and a willingness to learn. So, my fellow distillers, may your stills always be filled with ambition and inspiration. May your taste buds be forever delighted by the rich complexities you create. And may the spirit of home distilling ignite a passion within you that transcends the mere act of making spirits but encompasses a profound appreciation for the craftsmanship, the heritage, and the stories woven into every drop.